# Music Production, 2020 Edition

## The Advanced Guide on How to Produce for Music Producers (Music Business, Electronic Dance Music, EDM, Producing Music)

By Tommy Swindali

# Discover "How to Find Your Sound"

## http://musicprod.ontrapages.com/

## Swindali music coaching/Skype lessons.

Email djswindali@gmail.com for info and pricing

# Table of Contents

# Introduction

Everyone strives to be an authority or an expert in any or every one of their chosen careers or endeavors as the case may be. For this reason, nobody should be criticized but rather encouraged to be the best or one of the best in all their pursuits.

This scenario is not different in the music production scene. As a beginner strives to become a pro, a pro also strives to either retain that status or work harder to improve until he/she attains expert status. Before we delve into the intricacies of what it takes to excel in the music industry like a pro, we must establish exactly what professional music production entails.

## What Does Professional Music Production Entail?

Professional music production encompasses all the aspects, tangible and intangible tools needed to make great and hit worthy music. A pro music producer is tasked with either doing all the work or employing the services of professionals to do it while making sure a kind of synergy is established to produce the best results. Let us run through the various aspects of music production;

● The studio establishment aspects: getting a studio space, which may be at home or a rented space downtown, filling the space with the best budget-friendly equipment available, arranging the pieces of equipment in a way that will facilitate the optimal recording of songs, getting the best software, plug-ins and the likes.

● The creative aspects; talent hunt (budding music talents), music composition, songwriting, creating great music content, or employing the services of great music content creators.

● The engineering aspects; audio editing, analyzing sound recording, mixing, mastering, and exporting.

● The entrepreneurial aspects; publishing the recorded songs, marketing, and eventually selling the tracks to make a profit. This aspect also encompasses the legal and budgetary aspects of music production.

As a professional or aspiring professional music producer, your hands must be in all the cookie jars. This means that you must have an iota of knowledge about the above-outlined music production aspects. The fact that music production is a gradual process means you cannot be a jack of all trade just like that. This is where you have to precisely clarify what you want to achieve with your music production journey. A lot of people go into music production for various reasons; some go into it purely for the love of music, to make money, for fame and popularity, while others produce music just for fun. Regardless of your reasons, attaining pro status is not a child's play. It takes a lot of hard work, dedication, talent, creativity, and the ability to employ a few tricks (the tested and trusted by seasoned professionals).

Furthermore, professional music production entails recording a plethora of music types/styles for different purposes. It ranges from classical, jazz, hip pop, rock, country, pop to movie soundtracks, remixing, etc.

In the professional music and sound production scene, the major operational weapon is creativity and dedication. It is creativity and the ability to polish and fine-tune that differentiates an amateur music producer from a professional one. There is a need to go the extra mile with regards to equipment type, software type, studio space, studio time, and all other tools to achieve pro status.

## Objectives of the Book

The moment you have clarified and affirmed your music production end game, you need to work on maneuvering around present obstacles or downright eradicating them so you can achieve your goal as a pro music producer. One fact you should have at the back of your mind is that, if there is no synergy between your chosen music production strategy/technique and your music production end game, your career will be like a feather in a tornado.

One of the major obstacles faced by aspiring pro music producers in the rapidly and continually changing technology and applicable techniques. Another trending obstacle is the unwillingness to delegate the most technical aspects to the professionals. In this game, trying to be a jack of all trade will only lead to a substandard result, which is not your aim, right? For instance, the audio/sound engineering aspects require a lot of skill and experience, which you may not have at that time. What a professional does is to delegate, then supervise and push until you get that clean, clear, and rich sound you want.

Furthermore, we are in the digital era, the fast era. Making that killer music will definitely take a lot of time, patience, and dedication, which very few people have these days. At the end of the day, most upcoming independent music producers commence work on producing a track but end up giving up or not concluding well when things do not go their way, or the whole process starts to seem too slow. This is also an obstacle, albeit created by music producers' lack of discipline and commitment.

Therefore, the book seeks to teach you how to utilize your creativity and inborn talent in conjunction with textbook music production strategies and producer proven techniques in order to produce kick-ass music. Furthermore, the book promises to outline the best available software, music studio props, and equipment that are budget-friendly and, at the same time, facilitate efficiency. The main goal here is to show you how you can ramp up your skill level as much as possible so that you can make a place for your music in today's global music industry with emphasis on 2020 and beyond, help you make great mixes that sound cleaner and richer (marketable), and at the end of the day make great music.

Additionally, you will be provided with music production techniques that have been proven and vouched for by trending and reining authorities in pro music production with relevance to 2019 and the 2020s. Let us have a look at a number of these personalities that have made a name for themselves and their work in the music industry;

Robin Wesley; is a modern beatmaker whose career kick-started from simply having fun with a variety of music recording equipment and then posting it online. As a result of the popularity and feedback, he decided to make a career and ultimately money out of it by selling his beats to musicians, songwriters, and even record labels based on a concept known as beat licensing. Wesley was and is a staunch advocate of establishing synergy between music-making and music marketing (selling your work, investing in your effort) by giving both aspects an equal amount of hard work and focus.

YoungKio; is a 19-year-old young producer (beatmaker) of Dutch origins. He made major headway in his music production career when Lil X Nas used his beat to produce the musical marvel of 2019; ♫old town road♫.

Daniel Jimenez; started his journey right from his university days when he was inspired by Kendrick Lamar's album titled "DAMN." He is a staunch advocate of the saying, "practice makes perfect." He spent a lot of hours perfecting his craft by employing Anders Ericsson's deliberate practice technique, which paid off. The only area he fell short was not being able to achieve the same level of success he achieved in music-making in music marketing, which is very crucial and very relevant if you aim to succeed as a professional music producer in 2020.

The above mentioned successful professional music producers are just a few, among others. Their methods worked for them and made it possible for them to achieve success. No matter if you are a teacher, a student, or a freelancer, this book promises to provide you with ways to breathe lasting and marketable life to your music production ideas.

Yes, this book has promised to equip you with the weapons you need to be one of the best pro music producers; however, the book is not the holy grail of professional music production and therefore does not promise to encompass every and all the nitty-gritty of the subject. It is at this point, your willingness to exploit the web and other learning avenues traditional or otherwise (e.g., EDM podcast) will serve as a great benefit to you in your professional music production journey.

# Chapter One: The Professional Recording Studio

The consensus that before you can produce music professionally, you have to either buy studio time at a commercial recording studio or you cough out money which you may not have to open a professional music recording studio is no more tenable. Technology in the music industry and the current climate has advanced to such an extent that such a belief has been rendered mute. Basically, the caliber of sounds you produce does not depend majorly on the location or size of your studio anymore, what counts are your pieces of equipment, creativity, skills, and how you employ them to get the best. Without further ado, let us establish the various types of studios capable of producing professional-level sounds;

➢ Commercial recording studio

➢ Project recording studio

➢ Semi-pro recording studio

➢ Pro recording studio

➢ Home recording studio

Commercial recording studio

What makes commercial recording studios stand out is that they are set up in a way that accommodates various music styles and tastes to satisfy different potential clients, especially musicians.

For this reason, most commercial recording studios have large spaces with one or two much smaller carved out inner rooms for private sound recording and listening purposes. These carved out intimate control rooms allow for simultaneous recordings of different sounds that do not overlap or distort each other. How is this possible? These rooms are padded, paneled, and boarded with acoustic panels, soft wallboards, etc., so that sounds produced inside do not seep out, and at the same time, sounds produced outside do not filter in.

Even though commercial recording studios are structured in such a way that they are able to cater for the music needs of the general public (a plethora of different music personalities), they also vary based on a budget of the owners, the taste of the owners, and the target clientele.

An additional advantage of commercial recording studios is that it allows and caters to post music production activities such as music videos, movies, and TV conjunctions.

Even with all the edge promised by a commercial recording studio, they have become obsolete in recent times because of technological advancement. Technology has made it possible and quite easy to incorporate all the special attributes accrued to a commercial studio to a home recording studio space.

## Project Recording Studio

A project recording studio is like a general-purpose recording studio. It encompasses attributes of both commercial studios and home studios. Project studios' similarities with home studios can be attributed to the design, which gives it a homey feel. Project studios are constructed mostly for catering to the personal music recording goals of musicians, engineers, or music producers; however, it could easily be converted to a simple commercial facility, especially the ones not located at the home of the owner. Project studios are equipped with the most sophisticated audio production systems and studio equipment (drum machines, DAW, synthesizers, computers, samplers, synth modules, acoustics and a number of sequencing packages) that are capable of creating a plethora of unique sounds while simultaneously handling other music production undertakings such as audio editing, mixing, and mastering.

In the past, project recording studio cost a fortune to establish; however, with technological advancement and healthy competition in the music industry, they have now become very affordable and easily accessible to everyone, especially upcoming artists. In fact, it is safe to say that all home studios of the last decade exhibit the full capabilities of project studios.

## Semi-Pro Recording Studio

The characteristics of a semi-pro recording studio are synonymous with that of project recording studios and home recording studios (a cluster of rooms that are close together or jointed), in addition to the fact that it is structured and equipped with the necessary gear to accommodate numerous musicians recording tracks at the same time. Therefore, the semi-pro recording studio is highly recommended for musicians, engineers, and music producers who have future collaborations in the works.

## Pro Recording Studio

When you hear the words "pro recording studio," what comes to mind? A sizable structure dedicated solely to music recording with quite a number of rooms and several professionals running it right? Well, that is not all it is, it is so much more. As a result of the current speed of technological advancements and the promise of even more improvements in the future, you can as well make professional-level sounds in your home recording studio.

Furthermore, there are now online based professional recording studios that you could opt for. Although they cost a lot, many of them may not get the job done to your preferred standard, but some actually get very close.

## Home Recording Studio

As stated earlier, it not the size of the studio space or the "state of the art equipment" that dictates the quality of the music produced, although they also play major roles, the music production strategies/techniques adopted, productive time spent, and creativity of the artists, engineers, and other professional staff members are the main determinants.

While a commercial studio is a jack of all trade, a home recording studio is a jack of one trade. This means that home recording studio structures are direct reflections of the owners' music production end game (goals). Furthermore, these goals are determined by the following factors;

▪ Music taste; jazz, rock, hip-hop, orchestral, classical, etc.

▪ Skillset; a musician or music artist, audio engineering, and inborn talent.

▪ Budget.

- Short term and long-term goals.

- Willingness to collaborate with other musicians, engineers, and music producers.

As you must already know, attaining pro status in any field is not a cheap endeavor. It costs a lot of money. Money is one of the greatest obstacles afflicting budding musicians and the newbies in the music industry. Therefore, a professional or commercial recording studio seems like a farfetched/near impossible feat for a lot of upcoming musicians. At this point, what is left to be done is to touch up your home studio so that it is capable of producing professional-level sounds if you already have one. This can be achieved by upgrading your gear, software, plug-ins from beginner level music studio props to professional level props. Therefore, instead of continually pouring your limited cash into renting pro studio time, you can build your own custom-made pro home studio from scratch. It will serve as your first investment in your work and the first step you take in monetizing your craft, just as Wesley recommended.

Apart from the monetary benefits, there are other advantages that stem from working from home. Some of them include:

● You are the dictator of your studio time: Renting studio time in a commercial pro studio means you have to abide strictly by the opening and closing hours of the studio. For instance, if you suddenly get inspired, or an idea comes to you at midnight or any other odd hour, you would not be able to immediately work on it while it is still fresh because the studio is not available. However, if you had your own home studio, you would have the freedom to work on your music 24 hours a day if you like.

● A home studio presents you with the freedom to dictate what your workspace should look like. How a studio is decorated, such as paintings on the wall, the color of the walls, type of flowers, etc. may not seem important in the whole scheme of things; however, it helps to provide a tranquil and inspiring atmosphere. This is necessary for increased creativity and ultimately vital for making professional level sounds.

● Psychologically speaking, recording your music personally is highly recommended. It is said to help you build your confidence and grow into your music; then ultimately, you will be able to create and then hone your own unique sounds.

● Having a home studio makes it easier for you to carry out the regular purposeful practice. It makes available the ideal platform to set goals and makes it as easy as possible to achieve those goals.

## Reforming the Generic Home Studio into a Professional Music Capable Home Studio

In the first book of the series, which was especially for beginner and amateur music producers, what makes up a result-oriented home studio was explicitly outlined and explained. A lot of emphases were made on software and pieces of equipment that give the best result while being budget-friendly. The approach adopted was a sort of minimalist but effective approach. However, to be able to produce professionally, the minimalist approach is not an option. You have to go all out as much as your skill level, commitment level, and financial level allow.

In the generic home studio as clarified in book one, here are the components required;

– Computer; a laptop, a tab or a desktop

– Sound monitors; at least 2

– Headphones

– A Digital Audio Workstation (DAW) Software

– Microphones

– Audio interface/Sound card

– Optional studio props; Music instruments Digital interface (MIDI for short) keyboard, studio monitor stands, cables, Mic stands, and pop filters.

The above listed have been taken apart and explained with attention to detail in book one. Now for the professional music capable home studio, the following components are absolutely necessary. As we go deeper into the book, you will be well acquainted with the reasons why they are dubbed absolutely necessary, and the ideal quantity, quality, and specifications required. Therefore, the components for a professional home studio are made up of the items listed above and the following;

– Desktop workstation

– Studio chairs

– Both internal and third-party effect plug-ins

– Digital converters

– Bass traps

– Acoustic panels

– Acoustic diffusers

– Headphone amps

Note that all the equipment dubbed optional in book one such as mic stands, pop filters, monitor stands, etc. now become essential for that clean, clear, and rich professional level sound.

## Essential Human Components of a Pro Recording Studio

What makes a pro studio a pro studio are the actors, both human and non-human, and the capabilities of the actors. Most of the time, the emphasis is made mostly on the non-human component, but the human components are also very vital. In fact, they are more vital because, without skilled human components, the non-human ones become redundant as the case may be. Let us go through these actors and their roles in a professional recording studio

**The Artist:** The artist is the total package. He could be the songwriter or the lyricist or the musician. The artist is the component responsible for the level of creativity of the body of the song/track.

In a generic home studio, the common status quo is that one person (the owner) performs the functions of the songwriter, composer, lyricist, and musician. On the other hand, in a professional setting, several artists have to work together. The implication of this is that each activity is delegated to its corresponding professionals. In all settings, delegation facilitates efficiency and great outcomes.

For a professional music capable home studio, having all the actors present is almost an impossible feat. Therefore, what you can do is tap into the available music producer platforms on the web to get in touch with the creative personalities available there. Establish a link, maintain it, allow it to flourish, and you will get a double package deal. How? First, you are able to rub minds with talented people who will help you to improve as an artist. Secondly, you might be able to get your work done for free or at a very affordable rate.

**The Musicians and Arrangers**: if you want to be able to produce professionally in a home studio, collaboration must be part of your goals. If not short term, it must definitely be one of the long-term goals. To be frank, you cannot do it all by yourself. Being a loner will just not cut it because even those who have been years in the game and have all the experience need outside input, if not all the time, then occasionally.

Musicians are responsible for amalgamating the collective efforts of artists into a single to be reckoned with. Arrangers, on the other hand, are the ones armed with great knowledge of music theory. They are responsible for the placement of the notes, chords, scales, and keys, making sure the building blocks of the song are well placed within the whole song.

**The Producer**: The producer is the cool-headed persona in the studio. The producer is responsible for weathering any eventualities that occur and also making sure the overall process runs smoothly. In addition to making sure that the music production end game is achievable, the producer is also in charge of monetizing the end product. These monetization envelopes; meeting clients, sourcing for investors, etc.

Composers, songwriters or artists, in general, tend to get emotional and short-tempered when it comes to some aspects of their work. This may cause them to make decisions that may not conform to the artistic or commercial end game of the music. For this reason, the cool-headed and calculating persona of a good producer is crucial to mediate the situation. Therefore, there must be a modicum of trust and respect between the artist/musician and the producer, because their relationship in a recording studio is synonymous with the relationship between a roof and the pillar holding it up.

In some cases, the place of the producer and the audio engineer in the studio may become indistinct because they fit well into each other's shoes. The most common scenario in professional music capable home studios, the producer, the engineer, and sometimes the artist is just one person.

**The Engineer**: The engineer, as a human component of the music studio, is a highly technologically versed artist whose workload revolves around all that goes on in the control room. In a home studio, it is advisable for the engineer or the influence of the engineer to always be present at all stages of production. The reason for this is that a studio engineer is well informed in all the technological approaches that produce the best sounds possible. For instance, it is important for the engineer to be present during a recording session because he has the knowledge of how the microphones, the studio monitors, and other studio pieces of equipment are to be strategically placed for the optimum result. Furthermore, audio editing, overdubbing, mixing, mastering, sound importation, sound exportation, and even remixing are all within the work description of the engineer. The engineer's role in the studio does not cease at just tweaking, adjusting, and molding sounds into great masterpieces. The engineer also makes sure all the pieces of equipment (software and hardware) are in top-notch conditions so as to avoid disappointments and waste of time when they are needed.

**The Assistant Engineer**: The assistant engineer is basically an intern in the studio. He or she majorly assists the engineer in executing his or her duties. The longer he works as a protégé under the engineer, the better he becomes until he also becomes an authority too. If you are a novice and you are still struggling with the whole audio engineering shebang, serving as an assistant engineer in a well-established record label or under a well-known successful engineer, will get you far. You can then apply the knowledge gained in your own home studio so you can reform it into a professional music capable one.

**The Disc Jockey (DJ) and Video Jockey (VJ)**: The DJ is technically the marketer and the salesman charged with getting the finished music product to the general public. This is achieved via airwaves and the web, which is the most tenable and popular now. The VJ, in conjunction with the studio engineer, is charged with integrating images, videos, and the likes to the produced song. Music videos (good ones) complement the music, making it easily marketable and sellable, especially on the web. Music videos make songs more realistic and relatable, especially those that exhibit the exact message in the song.

Examine all that has been outlined above. Now ask yourself if it is feasible for one individual to efficiently fit into all the roles and efficiently carry out all the duties attached to those roles in order to produce professional-level music. The consensus is no and yes, which brings us to the next subtopic.

## Working with Others

The process of producing great music is an arduous one. It requires a lot of skills and technical know-how as the current climate of the music production scene dictates. It is extremely rare for one individual to have all the skills mastered. This is because these skills are very different, although some are dependent on the others; they require not just practice, online courses, and tutorials but also an experience that can only be gained by working with other actors in the community. Now, these actors might be your contemporaries or your seniors; the important thing is that you have someone or some people to run your work by, to give you a different opinion, and a fresh point of view. This might not seem so important; however, it is necessary if you want to produce songs that sound professional.

In the music scene, what does working with others entail exactly? It merely entails collaboration. Collaboration simply means two or more entities are working together to achieve a common goal. In the music industry, we have collaborations among musicians, artists, producers, engineers, DJs. Collaborations occur between actors of the same skill set (i.e., two or more musicians or producers, or engineers) and actors of varying skill sets (i.e., a musician and several engineers or a composer and a producer). One of the most important tools utilized by professional music producers is collaboration. It is quite a rewarding exercise if established in the right way.

# Types of Collaboration

In-person collaboration, as the name suggests, means that each party is physically present throughout the collaboration process. It is the fastest and most efficient method of collaboration.

Remote collaboration, as the name also suggests, means that each party is not physically present throughout the collaboration process. The particular benefit this method affords you is able to work with different people from different parts of the world. It is a slow method, but it gives you more dynamic options that will positively impact the overall creativity and uniqueness of your music.

The current trend in music has blurred the distinction between the two types of collaboration. How? The major cause is technological advancement. A case study will explain better how technological advancement has blurred the lines. Assuming there are three collaborating parties; a songwriter, a beatmaker, and a music producer. Do they all have to be physically present to achieve in-person collaboration? The answer is no because they all could be in remote places from each other (i.e., in different studios across the country or even outside the country) and still be physically communicating through video calls, Skype, and all other related internet platforms.

Collaboration works for professional production. A home studio is technically a solo set. Many home studio owners prefer working alone, but if you want to transcend from a generic home studio into a professional one, then collaboration is a tool that cannot be taken lightly. Therefore, if you are the owner or you aspire to be the owner of a professional music capable home studio, it must be at the top of both your short-term goal and long-term goal lists. Let us take a look at the benefits to your music that stem from collaborations.

## Advantages of Collaboration

### Ascending Creativity

It is rare for two different personalities to assess a situation in the exact same manner. Each assessment may either complement one another or contrast one another. Now, a contrasting situation may either yield positive or negative results. Therefore, in the positive light, music production collaborations culminate into an increase in the level of creativity and ultimately hit songs. Creative ideas from the participants of the collaboration are examined, fine-tuned, and refurbished into the best it can be. The final idea is then utilized in the production process.

### Platform to Build your Career

During a collaboration exercise, each participant has the opportunity to market his or her work to a new set of prospective clients and audiences. For instance, the collaboration between Lil X Nas (hip pop), Billy Ray Cyrus (country singer), and YoungKio (beatmaker) facilitated a geometric-like growth in the careers of each participant. YoungKio got discovered and was signed on by a reputable record label; Lil X Nas and Billy become more popular with fans of their respective genres and also fans of the other party's genre. In simple terms, Lil Nas gained country music fans to his fan base while Billy gained hip-pop fans to his fan base.

### Opportunity to Compensate for your Weaknesses and Amplify your Strengths

Every single person has weaknesses and strengths. It is now left to you to recognize them and find a way to balance them. In collaborations, one party's strength might be the others' weaknesses and vice versa. If you are the type who prefers to go solo at all times, then you won't get the opportunity to make use of your collaboration partner's strengths to reconcile your weaknesses. Collaborations also serve as check and balance, a way for you to be accountable so that you don't lax, and your commitment is intact.

## Exposure to New Techniques

In life, everyone goes through one experience or the other that teaches them one lesson or the other. Collaborations allow you to learn from both your mates and those that know more than you do as per music production skills.

## Effortless Delegation

Delegation of music recording tasks in the studio to the corresponding professionals facilitate work efficiency. Collaborations are a form of delegation. They make available a platform that allows every participant to concentrate on what they know best and excel in it.

# Chapter Two: Studio Design

At the beginner level of music production, not much emphasis was made on the studio design as a factor that significantly influences the quality of sound produced. Now that you are going pro, you need to pay more attention to details and not overlook any aspect of establishing the ideal studio. Why is studio design crucial to your end game? This is because the design of your studio informs the entry and exit of sound, the entry and exit of air and humidity into and from the studio, respectively, and the acoustics of the studio. Designing the ideal professional home studio is a painstaking process. It is an endeavor that requires a lot of time and more money than a beginner might want to spend on designing a generic home studio.

## First Step: Find a Professional Who Would be Involved from the Onset

This professional could be a seasoned record producer or a professional studio architect that will provide guidance, which will make your journey faster and smoother.

## Second Step: Select the Best Room or Rooms (Two or More)

The following series of advice and recommendations are based on the assumption that you are either aspiring to set up the studio at home or renting space outside your home. As a former beginner who is confident in his or her ability to be able to make professional-level music, it seems more logical for you to upgrade and renovate your already set up studio. Note that upgrading may also mean expanding it from just one room to two or more if you can afford it.

You must consider the following factors when selecting your studio space:

**Size:** your decision here is entirely dependent on what you have in terms of space and your budget. If you are not sure of the required size, then it is recommended that you get the biggest space you can afford because big sized rooms afford you the avenue to

– Cater to more than one musician, artist, an engineer at the same time.

– Have enough space to accommodate more sophisticated music studio props (e.g., drum kit) you subsequently add to your collection.

– Efficiently make clean, clear, and rich tracks.

**Proportion:** rooms that have straight lines both at the length and breadth create standing waves, which leads to interference (more on it later). What you can do is to bring in some furniture (useful ones) and place them strategically in the room (i.e., not clustered together). This helps to de-regularize the room to reduce the occurrence of standing waves to the barest minimum. In fact, it is much better if you can get a space with natural acoustics and irregular and unparalleled lines.

In addition, avoid spaces with dimensions that are multiples of the other; for instance, 18-foot by 27-foot with a 9-foot ceiling, because they lead to the amplification of reverberating frequencies that further culminates into an acoustic horror story.

**Surfaces**: In reference to the three major surfaces; the wall, the floor, and the ceiling, there some qualities you have to look out for.

In the case of the wall, avoid walls with full-length windows, mirror walls, and concrete walls. However, in the situation whereby you cannot avoid the don'ts, you have to be ready to carry out a considerable amount of acoustic treatments to reconcile the shortfalls.

For the flooring, the best option is hard wooden flooring although, tiled and concrete floorings also work albeit with additional trimmings to help them along. It is not advisable to lay carpets on the floors, as they only subsume high frequency and not low-frequency sounds which deter the effect of the acoustics, natural or otherwise. They also become worn very quickly as a result of foot traffic, scratches from moving pieces of equipment here and there, and heavy types of equipment. You can go for rugs instead.

Furthermore, if you are going to rent a space in a story building, opt for the ground floor to minimize the disturbance from foot noise.

For the ceiling, a high ceiling is recommended; actually, it is the best bet so that the full effect of any acoustic installation will manifest properly. Furthermore, high ceilings prevent the incidence of comb filtering that results from strong reflections during vocalization in the studio.

**Noise:** the incidence of noise is a two-way traffic which means that noise generated outside the studio such as rain, car honks, birds, wind, etc. causes disturbances that distorts recordings while noise generated within the studio such as vocals, piano sounds, drum beats, etc. causes disturbances to neighbors and other people not present in the studio. The problem has been established now how do you guide against it?

Make sure to choose a room far from the far eastern, western, northern, and southern parts of your home. It should be the most centralized room in the house to minimize entry and exit of sounds into and from the studio, respectively. If it is to be a rented space, try as much as possible to get one located in an uncongested neighborhood.

After you must have selected the room, make sure there are no cracks, holes, and dents anywhere in the room so that the effort put into selecting a quiet room is not defeated.

Life is not a bed of roses; therefore, do not presume everything will go as planned. In the event you are not able to get a very quiet location as a result of finances or unavailability, then you will have some soundproofing to do. How do you soundproof? It will also be explained later on.

### Third Step: Empty Out Selected Room

After you must have acquired the space either in your home or out of it, it is important to remove all unnecessary fixtures. It might be framed paintings, framed pictures, chandeliers, or any other decorative material that might cause vibrations. Unwanted vibrations are most likely to distort your recordings. Emptying the room is highly recommended because it is always better to begin work on a fresh canvas, which is what the cleared room is going to be. Moreover, if you are the type who likes to hang art pieces for one reason or the other (could be for creative inspiration), you can paint the empty room with any color of your choice, and then have a fine artiste draw paintings directly on the wall, that way there will be no vibration incidence, and everyone is happy.

**Fourth Step: Installation of Acoustic Treatment**

The next course of action after emptying out space/room(s) is to install the acoustic treatment. Acoustic treatment is carried out for two major reasons;

➤ To compensate for any issue that arises as a result of; room proportion, room size, and room location.

➤ To effectuate the ultimate environment necessary for recording clean, clear, and reach sounds.

Now that you are aware that the acoustics in a room also informs the quality of the recordings made in it, it will not do you any good to just go to the market to purchase just any acoustic material thereby wasting your money in the process; you need first to carry out a sound check to know the exact acoustic problem you have so you can then select the best way to treat it. Let us, first of all, go into more detail of the reason you need to carry out a soundcheck. A sound check will allow you to determine before the real recording starts; how the acoustics of the room will affect the sound and how accurate the sound recorded is represented, and in the event of any discrepancy, the steps you will need to take to correct it. For this reason, it is important to have the basic knowledge about the attributes of sound, how sound reacts when introduced to a room, the relationship between sound and the acoustics in a room, and the rudiments of acoustic treatment.

First of all, how do you carry out a soundcheck? The simplest way is to go for a tour of the studio space, making sure to test every spot, corner, or alcove. As you move around, make a sound by clapping your hands and stamping your feet. Listen carefully for the sonar feedback. A clap test will produce flutter echoes (harsh ring-like echoes). The magnitude of the flutter echoes will tell you if you simply need to hang heavy tapestries and place a few couches, or you have to go as far as changing the ceiling and flooring materials and hanging acoustic panels to treat the room acoustics. Of course, your budget will play a big role in determining the extent of your treatments. This method of soundcheck is quite informative; however, it doesn't give the full gist about how sound interacts with the structure of the room. If you require a more in-depth assessment, you can employ the pink noise test. To carry out this test, you will need an audio program capable of playing pink noise, at least two or more (as many as you can spare for the exercise) speakers strategically placed in the room and a frequency range analyzer. Pink noise is made up of all the sound frequencies in the auricular range played at the same volume. Thanks to advancement in technology, you can play pink noise on your smartphone and also analyze the frequency range simultaneously, using the corresponding applications. When you are ready to carry out the test, set the pink noise to play at a fairly loud volume, then move from one part of the room to the other while playing, make sure to note areas that produce flawed or faulty sound frequencies (i.e., the problem areas).

## Acoustic Treatment Versus Soundproofing

These two concepts are often mistaken for one another, especially in the novice community; although, they are two different concepts that cater to two different sound problems. Soundproofing is used to control the rate at which sound goes in and out of the studio either by reducing it or completely obliterating it while acoustic treatment is used to control the reflection, absorption, and transmission of sound within the studio space. Despite the differences in the two concepts, they are both required for better sound recordings that reflect professionalism.

## Let's Briefly Talk About How You Can Soundproof your Studio Space

If your studio is located in an isolated environment, you might not need soundproofing, especially if it is going to put a great strain on your budget. There are four processes you need to administer in order to soundproof the studio effectively;

1. Decoupling

2. Adding dense mass

3. Damping

4. Filling air gaps

**1. Decoupling**: this is simply to prevent vibrations produced by each equipment or surface when two or more pieces of equipment or surfaces are in direct contact with each other, from affecting the other. There is a reason why it is recommended for you not to place the studio monitors directly on the floor, directly on the desk or directly on top of each other. This is to prevent the transmission and amplification of vibrations and unnecessary noise, which negatively affects your recordings. Ductile materials such as foams, rubber pads, and the likes are placed between the surfaces to achieve decoupling. For the purpose of soundproofing, this action is applied to the entire studio space.

## Techniques

Duplicate the walls, ceiling, and floor. At the end of this, you end up with a room carved out of the original room. For the ceiling and the walls, you can make use of drywall, plasterboards, or sheetrock.

Installing the soundproofing material is where it gets tricky because it has to be installed such that bass vibrations would not penetrate into the room. How do you do that? Frame the original wall/ceiling vertically with a 2x4-inch wooden plank with a gap of 24 inches between each plank. Screw-in the whisper clips that will hold the resilient channels between the frame and the drywall. Install the drywall or any sound absorption material you wish to use. Make sure there is an air gap of half an inch between the drywall and frame, which prevents sound from entering and exiting the studio.

Float the floor. The floor is the strongest and fastest sound/vibration transmission medium; therefore, the sound created by all the pieces of equipment placed on the floor, such as microphone stand, drum kit, etc., will cause unwanted noise disturbances. You can prepare against that by laying thick rugs or mats to cover the entire expanse of the studio floor.

2. **Adding dense mass**: this activity is carried out before decoupling. It entails thickening the walls, so they do not react to sound waves. Concrete walls are mostly already dense and might not need additional mass. On the other hand, walls that are made from light materials will require additional mass. The most popular and easily assessable material for that is sheet block although, the most ideal is any paneling material that contains a fiberglass core. Thick walls either reflect sound or absorb it. They prevent sound from manifesting outside the boundary it is produced.

3. **Damping:** is a soundproofing method that converts kinetic energy produced by sound waves into heat. Damping techniques reinforce the effects of adding dense mass to the wall. Damping takes care of any residual bass vibrations from sound waves both from within and outside the studio space. Bass vibrations are really sneaky, no matter all the soundproofing already is done, they still slip through even the finest hairline cracks on the wall or ceiling to the microphone thereby distorting your recordings. This is why damping is very important, especially if you are going all out to do a thorough job. The green glue, which is one of the generally accepted damping agents, is used to completely seal up the wall and any spaces created as a result of the installment of wall frames and drywall. It is used to attach pieces of drywall to the wall frames and to another drywall. Have it at the back of your mind that if all these efforts do not completely remove the vibrations, it will slow it down so that its impact is greatly minimized.

4. **Filling air gaps**: this is the reconnaissance and double-checking stage. It might seem unnecessary, but the finishing touches done at this stage will crown all your soundproofing effort. Why wouldn't you want to do it? It is not expensive, it doesn't take time, and it is not difficult to do. What you simply need to do is go over all you have already done, fill up any leftover or overlooked air space such as; window seals, holes from the wiring, gaps from the plumbing pipes, gaps between the floor and the door as a result of elevating or floating the floor, and air condition vents. The tools used are foam gaskets, green glue, and door sweeps.

All these soundproofing's might seem a bit much such that you begin to assume there is no more need for acoustic treatment, but you are gravely mistaken. For a professional level gig, you have soundproofed as well as treat acoustic to make that superb sound you aspire to.

# The Rudiments of Acoustic Treatment

### How Does Sound Move in a Room?

When a sound is introduced into a room, the sound waves travel in two forms. Some parts of the waves travel in a straight line (direct sound) to the receiving point while the other parts are reflected (i.e., they bounce on all the available surfaces in the room) before landing on the final receiving point e.g., microphone. The direct sound does not bounce on any surface or is absorbed by any surface in the room; therefore, it is unadulterated. The reflected sound, on the other hand, is the reason for acoustic treatment. Reflected sounds in spaces that have been built from scratch with the rudiments of acoustic treatment are automatically controlled. It definitely would be fabulous to find a space already designed for acoustics, right? Unfortunately, such spaces are as scarce as they are expensive. Therefore, you have to make do with space you can afford and then treat the space to sound the way you want.

### What are the Acoustic Problems Precisely?

It is important to know the composition of the problems in detail so that you will be able to solve them effectively. The problems can be classified into three fundamental categories;

1. **Stationary waves as a result of interference**: stationary waves are just that, static. They are inert sound nodes that appear to be sitting in a spot when they are actually vibrating, albeit in one direction. Try to imagine what must have made droplets of water spill out of a cup when you place in on the table (or any other flat surface) after drinking. Can't you? Ok, I'll

explain. Immediately you placed the cup on the surface; there was a vibration generated from the center of the cup, which spread out to reflect against the edges of the cup and then converged back at the center, creating a force that causes the water to spill. This is exactly how standing waves behave in a room. It gets more complicated, the greater the room dimension.

2. **Modal ringing**: this acoustic problem arises when there are little to no absorptive surfaces in the room. It occurs in a resonance chain of reaction. This resonance greatly influences the sound frequency throughout the room, such that the whole room will vibrate at the same frequency as the initially generated sound frequency.

3. **Reverb times**: it encompasses problems of flutter echoes, unprecedented delay (i.e., not sanctioned by the engineer during audio editing and mixing), and maniacal sound reflection and reverberation, which is bad news for your recordings.

Now to the treatment proper! How can you go about solving the problems, especially those explained above? Each problem will require different treatment plans to solve them. However, each treatment falls under at least one of the following treatment plans;

➢ Brass traps

➢ Acoustic Clouds

➢ Diffusers

➢ Acoustic panels

**Bass traps**: bass traps take care of a great portion of the acoustic problems in a room. Some rooms do not need additional treatments once bass traps have been installed. Bass traps help to absorb medium, bass, and high sound frequencies. Bass traps are majorly installed at the corners, front, and back walls of a room that takes care of the modal ringing and reverb problem. Bass traps can be classified into; mobile and immobile bass traps

An example of an immobile bass trap is the super chunks (model reflection panels made from inflexible fiberglass), while that of a mobile bass trap is known as Gobos (good sound-absorbing capabilities). Gobos are used to isolate a portion of the studio for the purpose of recording vocals.

Super chunks are structured to stack the entirety of the room corners from floor to ceiling. They are also installed on the front and back walls of the studio vertically and horizontally to serve as the ideal reflection surfaces.

It is all good if you can afford to install bass traps at all the corners, the front wall, and the back walls of the room or at least the corners of the wall directly opposite your microphone stand or opposite the studio monitors. However, not everyone can afford it. With the assumption that you can only afford just one bass trap panel, and you can only install it in just one part of the room. The location to place it becomes the only problem that is actually easily solved. The best and most effective place to install the brass trap panel is the exact middle of the front wall. It should be installed in a vertical and horizontal position, and high enough to be parallel to your ears. This will also get the job done.

**Acoustic clouds**: when you go into some halls, restaurants, and hotel rooms, you will see a cloud-like structure hanging from the ceiling. If you were not previously aware of it, then know that it is not decorative. It is deliberately installed to prevent sound reflection between the floor and the ceiling. Therefore, it is made up of reflective acoustic panels. Unlike the bass traps that perform both reflection and absorption treatments, acoustic clouds only perform sound reflection treatments. Acoustic clouds become more vital in rooms with hardwood floors that have not been soundproofed with floating floors (i.e., rooms not covered with rugs or carpets).

**Diffuser**s: too much of anything is not good. Moderation is the best course to take, regardless of the type of activity you are into. If you are a well to do person, who has the ability to spare no expense on the design of your studio, then good for you, however, too much padding, paneling, covering, etc., will cause your recordings to sound lifeless and too artificial. For this reason, procuring and installing diffusers is a must as it helps to cure any issues that arise from such situations. What problem exactly do diffusers solve, and how are they different from bass traps and acoustic panels?

Absorbers are installed to minimize the great energy produced by some reflections, so they are not strictly focused within or stuck on particular frequencies. Diffusers, on the other hand, do not absorb a portion of the energy like the absorber panels; instead, they take in the whole energy then weaken it by distributing it evenly in different directions. Where is the best place to install the diffusers?

For small rooms, you most likely will not need diffusers. If the studio space is acceptably big, you definitely will need a diffuser. Place them at the front and back walls, preferably between the brass traps or reflection panels. If you can't afford more than one, place it at the front wall or the wall in the direction where the studio monitors will be facing.

There is a plethora of diffuser types (Quadratic, primitive-root, steeped, two-dimensional, and fractal), which may confuse you. The cheapest in the market today is the Quadratic diffusers; if not, you can opt for fractal diffusers. Apart from being affordable, quadratic diffusers are designed in random patterns that look like books of different sizes arranged in a bookshelf erratically. Randomly patterned diffusers are the best because they allow for very effective distribution of sound wave energies.

Going pro in the music-making community is not a cheap business. It actually devours money and time. Notwithstanding, there are always alternatives. They may not measure up to the standard, but they try. In the case of acoustic treatment, not everyone can afford sophisticated absorber panels or reflective panels, or other fancy acoustic panels. What you can do is install household materials that are absorptive such as pillows, couches, blankets, and mattresses. Furthermore, you have got to put in extra work (i.e., acquiring pieces of equipment that can be used to compensate for poor acoustics e.g., dynamic mics instead of the generally accepted condenser mics and reflection filters) during both your recording and mixing sessions.

### Fifth Step: Arrange your Gear

You have to know that you cannot just place your equipment, starting from your chair and workstation to the smallest cable, anyhow. You have to do it methodically to get the best of them. A lot more on the subject will be outlined in the subsequent chapters.

# Chapter Three: Setting up your Workstation and Record Station

The way your studio looks and how comfortable it is contributing to your output. Arranging your equipment to maximize output is also very important.

## For Your Workstation

Get a chair that promises comfort and will not put a strain on your neck and back as a result of sitting at one spot for long periods. A highly mobile chair (that can move around the room) and one that can rotate 360 degrees will be beneficial to you. The advantage derived from this is that you will be able to move around the studio without having to get up multiple times.

Get a work desk that fits the size of your studio, and that has a few pockets capable of housing some small pieces of equipment such as; the audio interface, the MIDI keyboard, and even a mini console. The advantage here is organization and space management.

### For Your Recording Station

The arrangement here should be directed by your music recording goals. There are two types of arrangement

One person only arrangement; this arrangement is the status quo in home studios where one person plays the role of a musician, producer, and engineer. The arrangement goes thus: set up your workstation at the center of the room, facing the front wall (can be also be referred to as the north of the room), arrange all other pieces of equipment such that they are in a circle around you. This makes it easy for you to switch between the roles.

Multiple persons arrangement; this arrangement calls for the division of the studio space into two stations. The first station will serve as the mixing and mastering session while the second (innermost) station will serve as the recording booth. Arrange your equipment accordingly. The set back to this arrangement is that there have to be two or more professionals at a time since one person can be at two places at a time.

Combination of the two; this arrangement enables one person to be in the two stations at once. How is this possible? Thanks to the DAW remote, you can be at the recording booth and still get things done on your computer, MIDI controllers, etc. simultaneously without having to bounce from one station to the other like a ping pong ball.

Now that we have established the studio arrangement, you need to know the type and caliber of computers, software, audio interface, and audio plug-ins that will facilitate the production of professional-level tracks.

## The Digital Audio Workstation (DAW)

The DAW is the engine that drives the music recording, editing, playback, mixing, and mastering processes. In the past, what was predominant was the console DAW type, it took a lot of studio space, but it was very efficient in producing professional-level songs. In recent times, the software-based DAWs are mostly used such that console DAW has been literally pushed out of the music production community. The DAW is a package deal comprising of;

– A kick-ass computer system (either Macintosh or Windows) that is strictly compatible with the DAW that will be installed on it.

– A DAW software of your preference that is capable of fulfilling your music needs.

– An audio interface/sound card.

The three outlined above are the primary components of the DAW. Here are the secondary components which are also important;

– Audio plug-ins

– Virtual instruments (VSTs)/MIDI controllers

Before, you select your DAW system; you need to make sure it has the following attributes;

Integration: your DAW system must be able to speak to and be spoken to by digital recording, editing, mixing, and mastering functions within the software package installed on it. The DAW must also be able to connect with external hardware and media export gadgets easily.

Speed and affability: DAWs becomes more natural to operate the more you use it. You can perform many of the functions in half the time it usually took to run.

Automation: unlike the analog system, the DAW affords you the opportunity to redo a session without losing data from previous sessions. Furthermore, every function becomes automatic once it has already been programmed into the system. That is the advantage of digital.

User-friendly: the operations in the DAW system must be straight forward and uncomplicated enough so the user, you, can operate it effortlessly.

## Now, to Take Apart the DAW Components One after the Other

The computer system; you must strive to get a computer with the following attributes

Speed: the processor is responsible for this. Get a computer with at least a fourth or fifth-generation Intel i5. If you can lay hands on an i7, that is even better. Know that your computer can never be too fast, therefore try as much as possible to get the fastest you can afford as much as possible

Memory: for a beginner, 8GB RAM is ideal, but you are going pro now, so you need to do better. Try as much as possible not to do lower than 16GB, so there is no room for problems arising later on.

Hard drive: apart from the hard drive that comes with the computer from the manufacturer, you will need an additional or two (if you can afford it) external hard drives. Get a 2TB minimum solid-state drive (SSD) with a 3.1 interface, a spindle speed of at least 7200 3Gg/s RPM, a seek time of at least 20 ms, and a 64MB buffer.

The DAW software: there are a plethora to choose from; those compatible with Macs, those compatible with windows and those compatible with both. After you must have selected your computer, then you need to select the digital audio software that is most compatible with it. Additionally, compatibility with audio plug-ins, your music production goal or end game, and of course, your budget also informs your DAW choice. Let us talk about the three-leading software for 2020.

## Ableton Live 10 Suite

➤ It is very compatible with live performances. This indicates that it is ideal for those with DJ and beat-making goals.

➤ It is a multi-track recording machine that records at not less than 32-bit & 192 kHz.

➤ Ableton live a MIDI with 10 virtual instruments and 41 internal audio effects.

➤ It is also packed with about 23 sound libraries with ingenious sounds of a capacity of over 50GB.

➤ It comes with a free trial package, so you can practice as you like.

➤ It is on the expensive side, as it costs about $800 online

FL Studio 20 Producer edition

➤ FL Studio 20 also comes with a free trial package.

➤ It is incorporated with great automation and mixing functions.

➤ It includes about 80 virtual instruments, including plug-in effects. Therefore, you do not need to buy it.

➤ One of FL Studio's edges over other DAWs is that it has the best piano roll.

➤ It is one of the most affordable. It costs about $200 online.

## Pro Tools HD 11 Audio Software

➤ This software is the most popular and generally accepted in professional circles.

➤ It is voted best for teachers and students of music production.

➤ Pro Tools includes about 60 virtual instruments and a plethora of sound libraries. Hence, it is superb for mixing and mastering functions

➤ Apart from recording and editing prowess, it is perfect for post-production activities. Therefore, it is one of the best options for VJs.

➤ Pro Tools communicate and integrate exceptionally well with external drives, plug-ins, and other external media gadgets required for import and export.

➤ It is slightly expensive too; it costs about $600 online. Notwithstanding, you need to really consider it because it is truly exceptional.

Other excellent and competing software are; Logic Pro X, PreSonus Studio One 4 Prime, and Reaper, among others.

The Audio interface: this piece of equipment facilitates sounds into your computer and out of it. Therefore, it works with all the equipment that input sounds into your computer, and those that transfer sound out of it into another medium. It connects through USB, XLR, FireWire, Thunderbolt, and PCI ports. It works hand in hand with your DAW software and computer.

Audio plug-ins: external plug-ins work with the audio interface to connect to the computer and, ultimately, the DAW. The internal ones (i.e., the plug-ins incorporated into the DAW) are synonymous with applications in a smartphone. They are very vital for mixing and mastering functions.

Virtual instruments (VSTs): if you are not part of a band or you work alone, you cannot joke with VSTs. With VSTs, you get access to a plethora of instruments that make it sound like the instruments are physically present in the studio. It is especially vital if your goal is beat making or a career as a DJ.

# Chapter Four: Equipment

There are two sides to a coin in music production, equipment representing one side, and talent serving the other. Having the talent or skills to produce good music is sometimes not enough; you also have to have the necessary equipment to match the skills. You are already familiar with some of the essential equipment required to produce music; this chapter will explore each type of equipment, highlight their specifications and discuss the features that make them ideal for certain types of music.

**Categories of Equipment that will be Discussed in this Chapter Include**

➤ Mixers

➤ Microphones

➤ Speakers

➤ Desks

➤ Subs

## 1. Mixers

An audio mixer sometimes referred to as mixing console, merges audio signals, processes them, and then routes (send) them out. With different technological innovations and advancements being released day after day, mixing is no longer restricted to just the big equipment placed on a desk in a studio. Now, with the right apps and up to date Android or iOS software, you can mix anywhere with your smartphone.

But for many producers and studio owners who are used to the conventional way of mixing music, nothing does it better than the dedicated knobs present on a hardware mixer. Choosing a mixer for your studio is dependent on these factors:

● Your budget,

● Working style, and

● The type of mixer you prefer.

The types of mixers covered in this chapter include:

➢ Recording /Live sound mixer

➢ DJ mixers

NB: The distinction between live sound and recording mixers isn't so clear because some mixers are capable of performing both functions effectively.

### Understanding the Features of your Mixer

The mixer is a very important instrument in music production, and the more familiar you are with it, the easier it is to produce music. You have to know the necessary ports to connect a mixer to the other equipment in the studio. Then you need to get accustomed to the different controls and configurations used to create different kinds of sounds. The glossary below will help you decipher all the features and educate you on how to use them.

### Channels

Channels are signal paths. Mixers with large channels allow for more connection and routing. Channels are constructed to accept connections with microphones, amplifiers, signal processors or preamps, and other lower-level and line-level devices. The number of channels and the features they come with differs, depending on the brand of the mixer.

## Channel Strip

This is a set of controls that make up each channel. A mixer is made up of numerous channel strips that allow you to route your signals when recording. Understanding how each channel strip works is not that hard; you only need to understand the basic makeup and operations of one to understand the others. The main job of the channel strip is to send signals from an instrument or mic to wherever the signal is needed. The channel strip or its layout varies in mixers, but its universal features are as follows:

**Input**: This is where you can select the input assigned to a particular channel; selecting this is as simple as choosing from a menu that opens on-screen; also, you can select it from your hardware interface.

**Output**: This button is used to control the output of your track; it can either be hardware output or that of the internal signal part available on the system.

**Automation Mode**: This button allows you to make a selection of the different automation modes available. In the digital system, automation means having your channel strip parameters such as mute, volume, panning, send, and insert level adjusted dynamically throughout a song.

**Track Group:** This option allows you to group your track with others; this is particularly useful when you are trying to create sub-mixes, i.e., a mixed track within a larger one.

**Panning Dial**: this dial or sliders, in some cases, can be used to pan your track to the left or right of the stereo field.

**Panning Display**: This allows you to see the panning position of your track, whether it is to the left, right, or center of the stereo field.

**Solo and Mute**: this button allows you to solo or mute a particular track.

**Record Enabled**: this function of this button is to enable a track for recording. It flashes red in all the recording systems, computer control surfaces, and digital mixers. The button is usually located on the physical unit and not on the screen.

**Volume Fader**: this button is for setting volume control for audios in a track.

**Volume Meter**: it is usually located beside Volume fader; it displays the volume of the track as the music plays.

**Track Type**: This comes in handy when you have a system that can record and playback audios and MIDI tracks.

**Numerical Volume**: it displays the volume of your track in decibels.

**Track Name**: This displays the name of a track to help you identify what is recorded in the track. Track naming is a common feature of many digital mixers. If you decide to change the name of your track, simply click on it and type in a new one.

### Input/Output

Input/output usually abbreviated as I/O indicates the number of devices that can be connected to a mixer. Before you can move your signal around within your mixer or carry out the necessary adjustment to it, there is a need to get the signals into your system. This can be done with input jack or trim control. There is no ideal number of inputs and outputs. The number of I/O you need depends on your plans for the mixer. In a situation where live sound mixing is needed, you would have to calculate the number of devices to be connected and get a mixer with enough inputs to accommodate the devices. You would also have to consider the number of speakers for output, but this rarely causes problems.

For studio mixing, it's another calculation entirely. The devices that would be part of the recording process and signal chain have to be accounted for. There are three basic types of input usually located at the back of the mixer

**Microphone**: The input for the microphone is known as the XLR input, often comes with phantom power as part of its connection; this is essential, especially for the condenser microphone.

**Line/instrument:** This can also be referred to as a ¼ -inch jack, it accepts line-level signals from a synthesizer and drum machine, it can also release a line-level output from your guitar amp

Hi-Z: is specially developed for the home recordist. An input of this type makes use of a mono ¼-inch (TS) jack that allows you to plug anything that has an electronic pickup straight into your system, giving you the liberty of not passing it through a direct box first.

**Trim Control**

This is a knob used to regulate the level of input signal entering the mixer. The trim control is usually situated at the top of the front panel of your hardware (SIAB, Digital, and Analog mixer). The instrument plugged in determines the adjustment of the trim control. Distortions are most likely to occur when the trim control is set too high also when set too low; you get a signal too weak to record, it is important to listen carefully as adjustments are being made.

Trim control has indications for line and microphone signals. The line signal is located to the right while the mic signal to the left, to get a clean sound into the mixer slowly turn the knob to the right for mic sources. Trim control can be used to adjust the level of recording; this is done by turning the control knob in an anti-clockwise direction, which in turn activates the internal preamp. This boosts the level of signal coming from the mic. Often times, the internal preamp of a mixer is moderately good; therefore, most professionals prefer to use an external preamp because they sound better or possess a particular sound.

**Buses**

A bus is best described as an intersection where outputs from multiple channels meet. Each channel in a mixer sends its signal to a particular bus or group of buses. The channel faders feed the master-mix bus, which routes the main output of the mixer to external devices like speakers and recorders. Auxiliary buses connected to channels are fed by the channel's volume controls. The aux buses route signals via their private output jacks.

**Groups**

Some mixers with large numbers of channels contain functions that allow you to regulate and process multiple channels simultaneously. Groups work like mini-mixers, with all channels being controlled by a fader and sharing a single signal processing and routing path. This way, the output sent to the master bus is more controlled.

## Inserts

Inserts allow for external sound processors such as equalizers and compressors to be connected to specific channels. This is usually done after the channel's preamp stage.

## Direct Output

This allows the preamplifier output of the mixer to be fed directly to external devices and recording systems.

## Cue System

This allows you to listen to the output of specific channels without altering the combined output of the mixer. The cue system's output is fed to a headphone or monitor speaker.

## The Difference Between Analog, Digital, and Software Mixers

While Analog mixers have existed since the dawn of recordings and public address systems, it was not until the early 1990s that digital mixers began making their way into the professional audio world. Over time, the capabilities of digital mixers increased, as well as their affordability. Analog and digital mixers are equally capable of producing high-quality sound; digital mixers are just fancier.

With the 21st century came the powerful computer and software-based mixers, some even more powerful than the regular digital and analog mixers.

**Analog Mixers**

This allows the routing of signals within the Analog domain. It tends to have a set of knobs, faders, and light for each channel. When you need to change from mixing input to mixing recorded sound, you plug and unplug cords or get a mixer that contains twice the amount of channel as your recorder.

Since analog mixing operations are controlled by physical faders, knobs, and switches, making their use more intuitive than digital and software operations. The physical controls also prove to be a major disadvantage as it's impossible to hide an analog mixer's signal and routing. In crowded studios and cramped places, it is easy to detect when the mixer is controlling and processing a signal.

Even with the invention of digital and software mixers, analog mixers still remain popular. This due to their affordability and simplicity. Some commercial studios simply prefer their analog mixers and their sounds. Besides, many engineers are used to the workflow of this analog mixer.

**Digital Mixers**

This type of mixer was designed to make life easy. Digital mixers perform the same functions and occupy less space than their analog counterparts. Once you know how to operate it, you perform music magic. Routing signals with this mixer can be as simple as pressing a button. You can switch from mixing input to mixing sound without the need to change any cord; all these are done in the digital domain. The probability of unwanted noise is less because there is no cord to mess with your work. Eventually, if there is a noise in the system, it is easier to find and eliminate it.

One of the most significant advantages of digital mixers is its ability to recall and store mixes. In the event that you have a stored programming route outputs and effects, you can mix and produce music without leaving a footprint. With the click of a button, you can have a bunch of effects that can't be detected like the case of analog mixers.

With the extensive capabilities and amazing flexibility possible on digital mixers, there is no wonder as to why it doesn't come cheap. To get a digital mixer, you have to be ready to spend, but you can be confident that your money was well spent.

**Software Mixers**

In terms of mobility and space, software mixers are unrivaled. They do not occupy actual in your studio; however, they may hold a lot of virtual space on your system, phone, or whatever device you have it installed in. You will also spend a lot of money purchasing access to the software as the good ones do not come free.

Software mixers can do just about anything digital and analog mixers can do. It offers you the features of a digital mixer but without its knob and faders. If you are looking for the flexibility of a digital mixer without the overwhelming need to touch faders and knobs, then this is the right option for you. It is usually a part of any audio or MIDI production software program and offers a variety of routing choices without the need for cables.

If you do not have much in terms of studio space, you should seriously consider this type of mixer. It may be difficult at first to grasp the mixing techniques, but with proper instructions and determination, you will understand the process.

## Live Sound and Recording Mixers

Packages of live sound equipment typically include microphones, main and monitor speakers, a powered mixer, speaker stands, and the cables necessary for connection. It's usually more affordable to purchase the equipment collectively rather than buying them individually.

With the same set of equipment, you will be able to achieve live sound and studio recording.

For DJ Mixing, you will have to get equipment that satisfies unique sets of needs. Not only will you need turntables and CD players, but you will also encounter difficulties trying to use a regular mixer to achieve a DJ mix. It's best to get DJ Mixers that are configured to handle DJ gears and connect with club sound systems.

## Factors to Take into Consideration when Purchasing a Mixer

To get a mixer that serves your purpose best, you need to consider the following questions.

## Application

– Are you using the mixer to play live, record, or DJ?

– Is the mixer rugged enough to handle the use you have planned for it?

## I/O and Channels

– How many microphones do you plan to connect to the mixer?

– Do the microphones have special requirements?

– Do your other forms of input have special requirements?

– Can the mixer satisfy those requirements?

– Buses and Signal Routing

– How many signal paths do you need?

– How flexible is the mixer's signaling path?

## Equalizer

– Does the mixer's satisfy your EQ requirements?

## Microphones

A microphone is a device that is used to convert sound vibrations present in the air to electronic signals. Microphones are used for different purposes; therefore, there are different types for different uses. Not all mics can be used in the recording studio, and a good microphone is a must-have in any recording studio.

Microphones can be grouped based on their construction, polarity pattern, and size of diaphragm.

## Classification of Microphones Based on Construction

Whether the microphone is as cheap as $10 or as expensive as $15,000, their primary function is to convert a sound wave to an electrical signal. Each microphone discussed in this chapter captures sound in its own unique way. Microphones can be classified into five categories based on construction:

➢ Condenser mic

➢ Dynamic mic

➢ Ribbon mic

➢ Boundary mic

➢ USB mic

**Condenser mic**: Mics in this category are usually well rounded and have a fast response rate because they operate on the electrostatic principle rather than the electromagnetic principle used in the ribbon and condenser mic. They are good at picking up high transient materials such as the initial attack of a drum. The capsule of a condenser mic is made of two plates; a thin moveable diaphragm and a fixed backplate. These two together form the condenser. The mic in this category has a natural sound to it, but be careful not to place them too close to the transient source, doing this makes them bring out a harsh sound.

**Dynamic mic**: they work on the principle of electromagnetic induction, which is used to generate their output signal, the mic in this category tends to accentuate the middle of the frequency spectrum, and this is due to their thick diaphragms. They are generally made up of a finely wrapped core of wire suspended within a high-level magnetic field that is attached to the diaphragm. When a sound wave hits the diaphragm surface, the attached coil is displaced relative to the proportion of the amplitude and frequency of the wave. Compared to the condenser mic, it takes a longer time to respond to frequency.

**Ribbon mic**: Mic in this group also uses the principle of electromagnetic induction, but are really slow in responding to an auditory signal. Due to this, they tend to soften the transient of an instrument. They contain a thin diaphragm, unlike their Dynamic counterpart. Their diaphragm is also suspended between two magnets.

Ribbon mic is not that popular because they are fragile and expensive, but they have a unique sound that is rich and smooth.

**Boundary mic**: They are similar to condenser mic and can capture a wide range of frequencies accurately, but they rely on the reflection of the sound source to a flat surface. This parallel setup allows the mic to pick up sound from the surface on which it is mounted, so when setting up this type of mic, you need to look for a surface that is large enough to reproduce the lowest frequency. Due to the difficulty in finding a flat surface large enough to reproduce its lowest frequency, they are mostly used for instruments and vocals that don't have a low pitch. One of the major advantages of this mic is that it can capture sound from multiple sources and in a reverberant room.

USB mic: These mics are excellent for producers on a low budget. They are not just cheap; they are also effective. With a USB mic, you can record a solo vocalist or an instrument, then connect a headphone or computer to it and listen. The use of long lengths of wire is immediately eliminated. All USB mics come with recording software, and it is particularly easy to connect it with a Digital Audio Workstation (DAW). They are pocket-sized and can be carried everywhere. The fact that they are small does not in any way reduce the quality of sound they produce. In fact, some USB mics allow the user to select the polarity pattern.

## Classification of Microphones Based on Polarity Pattern

The polarity pattern refers to different ways by which sound can be captured with a microphone. There are three categories under this classification;

➢ Omnidirectional mic

➢ Cardioid

➢ Bidirectional

Omnidirectional

From the word Omni, we can deduce that it picks up sound in all directions. This type of mic is useful when you want to capture both the source sound and the sound of the room that houses the source. They can't be used for source-miking as they tend to pick too much background sound.

## Cardioid

Cardioid picks sound in front of them but not the one coming from the back. This is particularly useful for live bands because the sound they pick can be controlled. There are also two types of cardioid microphones; hyper-cardioid and super-cardioid.

## Bidirectional

Bidirectional mic, according to their name, can only pick up sound from the front and back and not in all directions, unlike

Omnidirectional. Often times, it is used to record two instruments simultaneously. Bidirectional mics are also known as Figure-8 mics.

## Classification Based on the Size of the Diaphragm

Microphones use diaphragms to pick up sounds. The diaphragm, a thin material, vibrates when in contact with vibrations from a sound source. The diaphragm size of a mic affects the sensitivity, internal noise level, and the handling of sound's pressure level. Microphone diaphragms can be classified into three categories, small, medium, and large.

**Small diaphragm**: Due to their thin cylindrical shape, they are often referred to as pencil mics. They are compact, lightweight, ultra-responsive, and easy to position. Pencil mics are excellent for capturing sounds from musical instruments like acoustic guitars, cymbals, hi-hats, and other sharp transient instruments.

**Medium diaphragm**: Microphones with this type of diaphragm sometimes combine the features of both large and small diaphragm mics. They are able to produce full and warm sounds like those of large diaphragms and also have the ability to capture high-frequency contents as small diaphragms do.

**Large-diaphragm**: This type of diaphragm is popularly used in recording studios to record everything from vocals to instruments, room spaces, and various other sounds. Large-diaphragm mics are the leading choice for high-fidelity recording because they can capture sounds in great detail.

## 3. Studio Monitor/Speakers

Studio monitors have a huge role to play in the recording, mixing, and mastering stage of music production. They look incredibly similar to regular hi-fi speakers and home cinemas. You've probably come across a lot of them in home studios and mistaken them for regular speakers. Despite their looks, they are constructed to behave differently.

Hi-fi speakers and other regular speakers are designed to sound good, no matter the sound going through them. They possess features that allow them to modify sounds to sound good. The exact opposite happens for monitors. Monitors are designed for critical listening, so the music is played raw and without any refinement.

## Differences Between Studio Monitors and Regular Speakers

**Active/passive**: Hi-fi speakers and other home cinemas are passive and receive their power from an assigned standalone amplifier while studio monitors are active.

**Power amplifiers**: Active speakers usually have more than one power amplifier per unit, unlike passive speakers. The bass, treble, and midrange cones are powered individually in studio monitors making for a more detailed sound.

**Sound**: Studio monitors give flat and more precise sounds. There is no fine-tuning; hence the sounds played to give you an accurate impression of the mix, so corrections can be made when necessary. Even if the mix contains errors, regular speakers will make it sound good.

From the differences above, it's best you use a studio monitor for your recording, mixing, and mastering. Using regular speakers may lead you to miss some detail in the sound resulting in an imbalanced mix. Studio monitors can also be used as a regular speaker; the fact that it's designed for professional music production does not stop you from using it to watch TV.

**Types of Studio Monitor**

There are three types of studio speakers:

➢ Near-field

➢ Mid-field

➢ Far-field

**Near-field studio monitors**: These are small monitors designed to project sound to close distances. They are small enough to be placed or tables or desks beside the listeners. For effective listening, the listener has to stand close to the monitor as the sound waves it releases is not designed for bouncing off walls and ceilings. Near-field monitors have two kinds of the speaker, woofer, and tweeter. Because they are cost-effective and multipurpose, they are mostly used in home-studios.

**Mid-field studio monitors**: These types of monitors are usually bigger than near-field monitors and are optimized to project sounds in larger rooms. They also have two types of speakers, woofer, and tweeter. However, their woofers have 3-way designs and are significantly bigger than those of near-field monitors. Their larger woofers enable them to project higher quality sounds that fill larger studio rooms, so they don't have to be positioned close to the listener for effectiveness.

**Far-field studio monitors**: Monitors like these are usually used for live sound recordings in large halls or musical concerts.

In the construction of far-field monitors, more priority was placed on volume than acoustics. These stage speakers are loud and are usually used for fun listening as they are not really effective for listening to details. Far-field monitors have three types of speakers, low-range driver, mid-range driver, and tweeter.

## 4. Desks

The type of studio desk you have in your recording studio can either make life easy for you or difficult. It depends on the arrangement. A well-arranged studio desk boosts workflow by granting you access to the right gear at the right time. A cluttered desk is bound to slow down the production process and also make you develop a headache at the end of the day.

Some producers choose to make their studio desks themselves to enable them to have 100% control over the positioning. Producers that don't have the time or skill to make a desk resort to buying one. The price of a desk may range from about $500 to $6000, depending on the quality, durability, size, and functionality.

### Factors to Consider when Buying a Studio Desk

**Desk size**: The size of your studio dictates the size of the desk you can buy. It would be unreasonable to get a desk that occupies half of your studio space. Before you get a desk, go to your studio and measure the dimensions of the area, you want the desk to occupy. Have the dimensions in mind when you are buying or designing a studio desk.

**Gear Capacity**: How many gears do you intend to place on the table? What are their dimensions? Do you intend to buy more gears in the future? The questions will help you determine if the table is a fit for the present equipment you have and any future one you plan to add.

**Ergonomics and positioning**: Choose a desk whose arrangement supports and enhances your workflow. For instance, is the height of the desk proportionate to your height? Will you be able to access your gears easily with the angles of the desk? Is the studio monitor bridge close enough for optimum listening? All these questions are vital and should be considered when getting a desk.

**Build materials and design**: The quality of materials used to build the desk will affect the price of the desk. It will also affect the aesthetics, durability, and longevity of the desk. Carefully consider the design and build materials, and choose a desk that will serve you for years.

**Budget**: Quality studio desks don't come cheap. Getting one will sure dig a hole in your budget, so be suitably prepared.

### 5. Subs

Subwoofers, generally abbreviated as subs, are loudspeakers designed to give out low-pitched audio frequencies, such as bass and sub-bass, that generally have a lower frequency than the type of sound generated by woofers. Subwoofers have a frequency range of about 20-200 Hz. Subwoofers are sometimes called bass speakers.

There are two types of subwoofers- passive and active. Passive subwoofers are powered by external amplifiers, while active subwoofers have built-in amplifiers.

# Chapter Five: Professional Roles in Music Production

A lot of people want to get into music production, but they are unsure which part of the industry they fit into. They also don't know how to get from where they are to where they want to be. To advance in the music industry, you have to be aware of the requirements and the necessary steps. Examples of top careers in music production include

➤ Music Producer

➤ Sound Engineer

➤ Composer

➤ DJ, etc.

## Music Producer

A music producer composes, records, arranges, and produce songs. Basically, they are involved in all aspects of music production. Like a film director, the music producer gets to decide which artist to record, how the instruments are played, the vocals to be featured in the song, and the location the song is recorded.

All major decisions concerning a song are taken by the music producer; therefore, he must be able to convey his vision of the final song to the other players involved in producing a song. Those players include audio engineer, mixing engineer, mastering engineer, vocalists, and various other technicians.

A music producer also has to be proactive and plan in advance to prevent scheduling conflicts with recording session players. It will not do book an emergency recording session when the backup singers or lead vocalist is unavailable.

The job also requires great communication skills and the ability to understand logistics and budgeting. Generally, the duties of a music producer include the following.

– Responsible for scheduling the studio sessions until all production work is done

– In charge of the acquisition of instruments for production

– Hires the necessary studio players and negotiates their fees

– Monitors the spending and release of funds

– Guide and coach musicians when necessary

– Create quality sounds that fulfill both the producer's and the musician's vision.

– Assist the sound engineers with the mixing and mastering process (in small record labels that are unable to hire a sound engineer, the music producer takes over the duty).

– Makes sure that the entire production process is done within the budget.

The numerous duties listed above are only done by upcoming music producers. You won't have to carry out all these duties when you become a top-shot producer. Then you will have the funds to hire more studio players and experts to lessen your workload.

## Educational Requirement of a Music Producer

A bachelor's degree in fine arts, sound engineering, and music production are beneficial but not compulsory for a music producer. An interest in music and passion for creating jams are the key qualities of a music producer. No one is going to reject you because you don't have a degree in music production or music business.

While it is not necessarily important that you have a degree, lack of experience in music production may be a deal-breaker when job-hunting. You can get experience by taking a course in a music school or interning in an established record studio.

## Career Advancement

All careers in music production are extremely competitive. Advancements only come after a music producer has established his skill set and can land gigs with prestigious artists. A lot of top-shot producers began at home and got to where they are by generating buzz with a mix made in their home studio.

There is no guaranteed success in the music industry. With the industry fuller than ever, it's going to be extremely difficult to break-in. Some artiste and producers spend years releasing mixes and demos before they get noticed.

Music producers have average annual earnings of $49,000 and a general earning of $25,000 to $1,000,000. The money is good, but before you can start earning good money, you have to make a wave.

# Sound Engineer

Sound engineers, also known as audio engineers, play a critical role in the music industry. Have you ever been to a concert and wondered who was responsible for the overall clarity and quality of the music? Well, the sound was controlled by a sound engineer. They are responsible for mixing, reproducing, and manipulating the electronic and equalization effects of sound.

As engineers, they do not necessarily have to stick to music. They are also capable of handling sounds at conferences, theaters, and other events that require sound projection. They control the microphones, adjust sound levels, control output, and with their well-trained ears and knowledge of acoustics, are able to produce quality sound for numerous purposes.

## Examples of Projects a Sound Engineer can Undertake

➢ Radio

➢ Film

➢ Computer games

➢ Television

➢ Corporate events

➢ Sporting events

➢ Theater

## Specializations in Sound Engineering

As you must know by now, there are four separate steps involved in the commercial production of music – recording, mixing, editing, and mastering. Because of this, there are several sound engineers with specializations in different steps. A single sound engineer can handle all four stages, especially when specialized sound engineers can't be hired. Usually, separate sound engineers are only hired for well-funded events and tours.

## Specializations Include

System engineers: Sound engineers in this category are in charge of setting up speakers, amps, and complex public address systems for bands.

Monitor sound engineers: These engineers are in charge of the sound produced by stage monitors. When a band member says, "can you lower the volume of my guitar?" the statement is meant for the monitor engineer.

Research and development sound engineers: These are engineers that invent new techniques and equipment to enhance the art of sound engineering.

Wireless microphone sound engineers: They handle the miking and feedback of wireless mics used in sporting events, corporate events, and other types of live events.

Game design sound engineers: Engineers in this category help with the creation and development of theme music for games. They are also responsible for the balance of the other sounds used in games.

Mixing engineers: Responsible for the "mixing and combination" of the different sonic elements of recorded vocals, effects, and instruments into a song/mix. They are responsible for the balance, volume, positioning, and effects of the song. Sometimes their duty is shared with the music producer.

Mastering engineers: These engineers take over from the mix engineers. They work on the mix produced and prepare it for distribution. The mastering engineer corrects any imbalance that escapes the notice of the mix engineer and makes the mix/song ready for listening.

Sound Designer: A sound designer has to search for recorded or live sounds that can be used as effects during music production. Not all sounds for music used are recorded in the studio. The sound designer procures them from their source and cleans the sound for use in the studio.

Some producers or mixers serve as their very own sound designer. However, if they are unable to get the particular sound they need, they hire a sound designer or buy the sound from platforms owned by sound designers.

## Educational Requirement of a Sound Engineer

Many universities and music schools offer specific training in sound engineering. To land a job as a sound engineer, you need to get some sort of training and have some years of experience.

## Career Advancement

Sound engineers have average annual earnings of $43,660 and a general earning of $ 20,000 to $300,000. The US Bureau of Labor service projected that job opportunities in sound engineering would grow by 8% in the next decade. This is far higher than the 5% projected for other careers in the music industry. The reason for the higher value is because sound engineers can work in industries that are separate from music.

# Composer

A composer is a person that creates and organizes the flow of original music used in various parts of the music and film industry. They are responsible for creating sound recordings that convey stories in film, audio, and video games. They also have to tell the stories skillfully so it will not distract the viewer.

Have you ever wondered about the importance of music in movies and video games? Blockbuster movies/series like Fast and Furious and Game of Thrones employed composers to create scores that match the mood of the movie. Not all scores have to contain lyrics; most of them are just combinations of various musical instruments. A perfect example of such a score is The Game of Thrones theme music. It was composed by Ramin Djawadi and had cello as its main instrument. Another score composed by him that was equally popular was the Light of the Seven scores that played at the beginning of show's season 6 season finale. The score was created with piano, cello, and vocals, and it perfectly expressed the tragedy that would later occur in the episode. Some viewers even claimed that the score alerted them that something huge was about to happen. That is the work of a composer to create flawless sounds that are capable of expressing emotions to the listener.

## Projects that Require the Skills of a Composer

➢ Movies

➢ Television shows

➢ Orchestra

➢ Commercials

- Songs

- Plays

- Video games, etc.

# Songwriter

A songwriter is also a composer, but a composer who writes songs. A songwriter is more focused on the lyrics of the song than the complete combination of vocals, instruments, and effects that make up a song.

## Educational Requirement of a Composer

Schooling is vital for composers. It's important for them to understand the basic mechanics of music. A degree from a university or training from a music school will suffice. Apart from education, there is a need to have a natural talent and passion for music.

## Career Advancement

The advancement of composers comes with skills and networking. The nature of their work does not allow them to stay on a project for long. Once they are done with a project, they will need to apply for another job. And if they execute their previous project excellently, the employer may hire them again or refer them to a friend.

Composers have flexibility over their pay as they have the opportunity to charge per hour or per contract. Some composers charge as high as $60 per hour and can work as much as a thousand hours on a single project. Their work can be done in a small home studio, but it must be able to record the necessary instruments and sounds.

Mid-level composers earn an average annual salary of $50,000 while beginners in the career start with a yearly salary of about $20,000.

# Disc Jockey (DJ)

Disc jockeys, or deejays as they are popularly called, are responsible for the combination of sounds and music we hear at parties or on the radio. They are real-life at the party! Because, if the DJ can't get the crowd to groove with him, the party is sure not going to last for long. A lot of work goes into the production of sound the DJ plays. A good DJ has to know how to mix, master, and edit sounds. Playing and remixing already created songs can get a bit boring after a while; a DJ needs to be able to create his own beats and effects.

Events that hire a DJ

➢ Birthday bashes

➢ Night parties

➢ Bands

➢ Dance competitions, etc.

## Educational Requirements

There are no school programs or degrees for DJing. Most DJs are self-taught. After a few years of playing around, some DJs do go to music school to learn more, especially those with interest in producing beats for artists.

## Career Advancement

The competition for DJs out there is stiff. There are always a couple of upcoming DJs hanging around clubs hoping to get an opportunity to showcase their talents. The early days of DJing are always tough because they only get the chance to play on weekdays, days with a small crowd, while the top-shots get to own the weekend parties. Even then, beginners are not usually paid, but if they are lucky, they may be able to get some free drinks and entry vouchers.

The selling point of most DJs is their personality. Some are skilled enough to incorporate it into their sounds. People that hear such sounds and like it become fans. DJs need a fanbase to advance in their careers. It's the fans that encourage club owners or party planners to hire a particular DJ.

Networking is also very important in DJing. Most DJs get their jobs through referrals and reviews of previous clients or acquaintances. DJs also have to employ the services of bookers and promoters to help them get jobs and manage their schedules.

Once they start getting recognized and are able to get a fan base, the money will start flowing in. Upcoming DJs are paid about $500-1000 per night, and for top shot DJs like DJ Khalid, the sky is the limit.

In general, the average annual earnings a DJ is about $30,000.

## Your Career Choice

After reading about the careers listed above, you must have a few questions on your mind. Questions like, "Which career is more related to your interest and passion?", "Can you possibly have two or more of these careers at the same time?" "Can you use the skills you've learned so far with this book series to start or continue one of the careers?" "Where do I start from if I want to start producing music now?"

## Which Career is More Related to your Interest and Passion?

This question can only be answered by you. It's quite clear that you are interested in producing music because you are reading this book. But what aspect of music production are you passionate about? Try to download free software to practice. While practicing, you will definitely find the aspect that comes really easy for you. Develop yourself in that aspect and choose a career that revolves around that aspect. For example, if you are talented at controlling the flow of music and brilliantly combining them, you should consider choosing DJing as a career.

Once you can identify your interest and passion in music production, choosing a career won't be so difficult.

## Can you Possibly have Two or More of these Careers at the Same Time?

It's possible to have two different careers at the same time, especially when starting in music production. You would have to go back to the beginning and try your hand at different careers, then stick to the one that suits you the most. For example, you can be a DJ, a composer, and a music producer all at the same time. The workload may be discouraging at first, but with the time, you will find the one that gives you the most fulfillment.

## Can you use the Skills you've Learned so Far with this Book Series to Start One of the Careers?

Yes! The purpose of this series is to equip with enough technical knowledge to attempt or continue any of the careers. It would be a waste if you completed the books and are unable to attempt anything in music production. So, feel free and pick a career.

## Where do I Start from if I want to Start Producing Music Now?

Start from scratch. Get the necessary software and some equipment, if you can afford it, and start practicing. Develop your skills enough to produce a professional mix. When you think you are ready to share your talent with the world, create an Instagram page for your sounds. Or better still, send your mix to DJs or music producers that are friends and ask them to review the sound. The reviews and comments you get from your Instagram page and friends will help you improve on your sound, and when you are good enough, you may get invited to help produce a sound for a project. That's how Robin Wesley did, so you can! The key is starting immediately. Start now and start small, but think big!

# Chapter Six: Making a Hit

Truthfully, there is no blueprint for creating a hit record. Thousands of tracks are released daily. But only a few manage to make it to the top. Studying those few fortunate ones lies the clue to producing a hit. This chapter will dissect a popular 2019 hit sounds and help you recognize what you need to add and improve on in your sounds to make it get recognized in 2020. As a music producer or enthusiast, analyzing tracks of popular artists can be an eye-opening exercise.

## Structure and Arrangement of Recent Songs

Most of the songs that popped in 2019 followed the same arrangement tactics that have been popular for a while. The arrangement used satisfied our modern need for a "quick fix." For example, the lengths of all the 2019 billboard songs were between 2.30 to 3.30 minutes. The days when people actually sat and listened to songs of about 6 to 7 minutes are long gone. Just as the world is moving fast, so are the songs being played.

A breakdown of activities done within the average length of 3 minutes shows that the intro of the hits last less than 15 seconds and immediately after comes the 1st chorus. A good reason for this is that most listeners decide whether they like a song or not within the first 30 seconds, and if the intro and chorus are not solid enough to attract their attention, they may skip it for another song. Not all hits followed this tactic; some delivered the first verse immediately after the intro. But even with the verse coming first, it was noticed that the producers found a way to incorporate the 1st chorus into the song within the first 60 seconds.

With the intro, chorus, and verse, the songs were able to attract the attention of the listener; however, keeping that attention was another matter entirely. People today have a short and flaky attention span and will need a reason to keep listening. Songs that we're able to change things up after the first minute kept their listeners hooked. The changes were mild with a few additional harmonies, groove changes, and addition/removal of sound effects every four bars. All-in-all, the flow of the song had to be steady and attractive.

Previously, hip-hop hits used to have 16 bar verses and 8 bar hooks/choruses, but now, 12 bar verses and 8 bar choruses are making the waves. In 2020, new trends will rise with people listen to songs with more beats than lyrics.

– The general structure of recent hit songs includes:

– A short intro

– A couple of verse and choruses, and possibly a pre-chorus

– A bridge-like departure session

– A climax featuring the highest amount of energy

– A thrilling outro

## Sounds and Moods that will Trend in 2020

Based on the sounds and moods that trended in 2019, analyst speculates that some of the songs that will trend in 2020 will contain

– Pronounced sub-bass instruments

– Bouncy drum grooves

– Slow tempos recorded for a 70bpm feel at 140bpm

– Fast and rolling hi-hats

– Dark melodies

– Minor melodies

Incorporating everything discussed in this chapter into a mix will not give you 100% assurance of a hit. The trends discussed are based on hits already existing. Once in a while, unique beats that are different from the trend are able to make it to the top. When making your music, don't aim to replicate a famous hit song, make the sound yours and give it your personal feel.

## The Production Process

To explain the production process explicitly, the stages of production will be split into six stages rather than the four used in previous chapters. The six stages are:

1. Songwriting

2. Arranging

3. Tracking

4. Editing

5. Mixing

6. Mastering

### 1. Songwriting

This stage involves the combination of musical ideas to form a bigger structure of audible harmony, melody, and rhythm. The lyrics and the music instrument to be used in a song are determined in this stage. The producer or songwriter/composer envisions what he wants the song to sound like and writes it down in a score.

## 2. Arranging

The arrangement and coordination of the beat are done here. For example, when the melody of a beat is too repetitive, the problem is identified here and rectified. Some producers do skip this stage, despite its importance.

The arrangement is mainly concerned with the timeline of the song. It allows you to see the attractiveness of the intro, the buildup of the lyrics and melody, and the arrangements of the instruments used for the song.

## 3. Tracking

Some producers refer to this stage as recording. This is where the recording of the various sounds that will be showcased in the song is recorded. The sounds are usually recorded individually to ensure its quality. Every time a track is recorded, it is played in combination with the other tracks to ensure that it is following the right format.

Some people do combine the tracking process with the songwriting process, but to ensure efficiently, it is best done separately.

## 4. Editing

This is a crucial stage in the music production process. It should not be combined with any other process and should command the full attention of the editor or producer.

The goal of this stage is to make the recorded performance sound as good as possible. Parts that are okay without editing should be marked as no-go-areas, while parts that require attention should be edited appropriately.

## 5. Mixing

For many, the fun starts here. The song has been written; the parts have been recorded and edited, now is the time to sit back, relax, and transform the raw song into a masterpiece. Mixing is the most interesting and, by far, the hardest part of music production. What happens here determines how far the track goes. Before you can create a hit track, you need to have years of experience from practicing and learning.

A carefully crafted mix will allow the listener to hear all the instruments and vocals recorded clearly without crowding the sounds. Mixers get to choose the instruments that are more pronounced, the sounds that get to play upfront or in the background, and the type of effects that are used. This stage comes with a lot of pressure and complex decision making because it can make or mar the attractiveness of the sound.

A lot of people focus majorly on this aspect and pay little attention to the other parts of music production. That is unwise because every single stage in the production process has a role to play in the final sound produced at the end of the day.

## 6. Mastering

This is the final stage in music production. Any error missed by the mixing engineer is corrected in this stage. Any final tuning left to be done on the track is completed here. Basically, the proofreading of the sound and effects are done here, before it is published for listening.

More on the production process will be explained in Chapter Seven.

## Working with Bands or Working Solo

Whether you are working with a solo artist or working with a band, the entire production process is the same. All artists/band members participate in the songwriting and tracking process. Even if the song is not written by the artists, they have to participate in the songwriting stage to fashion the lyrics according to their vocals and style. Sometimes, they will rewrite it to sound more like them.

The editing, arranging, and tracking processes are managed by the producer, and in situations where the artist or band members are unable to hire a mixing engineer, the producer will take on the role and edit the song until it is ready for the listeners. It is also possible for the artist to get involved in the mixing and mastering process if said artiste has some experience in creating and editing sounds. It will make the tracking process more straightforward because the artist will be able to share the vision of the final song and nail the necessary vocals quickly.

# Chapter Seven: Production Technique

The production techniques employed can also determine whether a song would be a hit or not. As it was discussed in the previous chapter, the intro of a song and the arrangement all work together in creating a piece of music that may go on to be a hit. Producing music is synonymous with a painter combining different colors together to create a beautiful masterpiece.

There are so many things involved in creating good music that listeners get addicted to; most times, it is more than just using the trending structure and moods. Here is a tip that will not only help in improving your sound but will also get listeners hooked to your song.

➢ Make use of a good sound source: Using a good sound source will make your life easier. Now the question is, how do you get a good source sound? It starts with your audio sampling. Become your very own sound designer. Scout your sounds and get creative with the sounds you hear in your natural environment. Find rhythm in movements taking place around you. Who knows, it may just be the sound that will boost your career and make you go viral.

NB: Remember to use the noise reduction techniques explained in chapter two while recording your sounds and make sure you record them separately, so no distortion occurs.

## Techniques in Music Production

Two major techniques = in music production would be discussed explicitly in this chapter. They are;

➢ Sequencing

➢ Layering

## Sequencing

Sequencing in music production is the process of recording, editing, storing, and playing back a MIDI data. A sequencer is a hardware or software that can be used to carry out these functions (sequencing). Sequencer software includes Pro Tools, Digital Performer, and Cubase. Nowadays, not only is a sequencer able to record an audio or MIDI data, but it can also be used to store audio information. This helps you to create complex arrangements, including synthesizing the MIDI track and acoustic track at the same time. Being able to achieve this makes it possible to improve the timbre of the sample and synthesize sound. The signal path followed by the MIDI and audio data is different, and it's crucial that you understand this difference. Audio data reaches the computer through an audio interface, while the MIDI achieves this through the MIDI interface. Most sequencers are designed to work in a way similar to the multi-track tape recorder, but like multi-track recorders, each track can be erased, copied, and re-recorded. Software sequencer is way better than its hardware counterpart due to its speed and flexibility.

Below are the advantages of software sequencer over their hardware counterpart

➤ It has the ability to change notes, one at a time or over a defined range.

➤ Performance timing can be easily adjusted.

➤ Easy adjustment of tempo within a session.

➤ Saving and recalling a file is very easy.

➤ There is an increase in graphics capability.

Well, one important thing to know is that a sequencer does not store sound directly; instead, the MIDI messages the instrument, instructing it as to what note is being played, what channel it's going to pass through, and its velocity.

How a sequencer works

➤ Recording

Whether hardware or software, a sequencer is designed to emulate a traditional multitrack-based environment through a working interface. A set of transport controls allows the movement from one location to another using the standard record, play, fast forward, and rewind command buttons. Besides, after using the record button to select which track you want to record, the next step is to select the MIDI input port (the source), output port (the destination), and the MIDI channel.

## Editing

It is one of the most important features of a sequencer. The ability to edit track varies in each sequencer. The main track window of a sequencer on a DAW displays information like track name, track data, and other commands. The best way to understand sequencing is to experiment with your setup. This section will cover some basic techniques employed when you are sequencing your own music.

## Basic Editing Techniques

▪ **Transposition**: This is the process of changing the pitch or the entire note of a track. Transposition is very easy to achieve with a sequencer, depending on the type of system you are using. A song can be transposed up, and the pitch downed (lowered). Transposition can be performed on a whole song or just a segment, by calling up the transposed function from the program menu.

- **Quantization**: This is the process of correcting timing errors. It allows those timing inaccuracies to be fixed and adjusted to the nearest musical time-division e.g., the quarter, eighth, and sixteenth notes. For instance, when performing a passage that needs all its note to fall exactly on the quarter-note beat, a mistake can easily occur. Once this happens, the problematic passage can be recalculated by the sequencer to such that each note starts and stop on the boundary of the closest division time.

- `Slipping time`: This is one of the timing variables. It works by moving a selected range of note either forward or backward in time by a defined number of clock pulses, or it helps to change the timing element in a sequence. It also changes the start time of these notes.

- **Humanizing**: This is simply the random alteration of all notes in a selected segment using parameters such as note duration, velocity, and timing. The amount of accidental alteration that occurs can be limited to a percentage range, and the parameters can be individually selected or fine-tuned. This randomization process can help add expression to your track.

- `Playback:` After composing and saving your sequence to a disk, it is then transmitted through various MIDI port and channel to devices to make music. MIDI exists as an encoded file and not as audio, and this makes it possible to make changes to the sequence at any time. In the studio, it is now a norm for MIDI tracks to be recorded and played back in sync with a DAW, analog, or digital multi-track machine. When there is a need for more playback in production, a process known as synchronization is employed to ensure that this event occurs at the same time. Synchronization can be accomplished in various ways depending on the device used.

• **Saving your files**: It is very crucial to backup and saves your session files while in production. Saving of files can be done in two ways. The first method requires you to save your files over the course of production periodically. To better achieve this, you can set up a program that will automatically carry out these functions at regular intervals. The second method involves the saving of files at specific points throughout production. For that, you may save your file with specific names that make it possible to easily revert back to the saved point if there is a need for any adjustment.

NB: Always save the original MIDI file. A MIDI file can be converted and saved as standard MIDI format files, which can be exported, imported, and distributed for use. These files can be saved in two formats:

o **Type 0**: All MIDI data within a session are saved as a single MIDI track while the original MIDI channel number is retained.

o **Type 1**: All MIDI data within a session are saved onto separate MIDI tracks that can be easily imported into a sequencer.

**Layering**

This is the process of stacking several similar sounds with slight differences together, to create a unique sound. It is one of the most critical skills to acquire in music production. Layering is not without its own benefits as it is a smart way of creating a signature sound, rather than using pre-set which is popularly used. However, layering is not just about stacking any sound upon each other; it requires the careful addition of different elements, which are added for a specific reason.

## How to Properly Layer a Sound

Before you can layer a song, there are three major characteristics of the sound you must carefully put into consideration. These characteristics are

➢ Frequency or tone

➢ Transients or dynamics

➢ Stereo field

The first two must be carried out in mono; doing this will help you detect whether your layers are experiencing a phase issue.

**Frequency/ tone**: Different instruments are made up of different frequency ranges; therefore, you need to be careful when layering so that frequency-wise, they are not clashing. The key is selecting the right sound. You can use the spectrum analyzer to check whether each layer is crashing in the frequency spectrum. You can also use the reductive EQ to create space for each layer.

**Transients/ dynamics**: The dynamic characteristics of a sound can be defined by parameters such as attack, decay, release, and sustain. The layering of sounds with different dynamics gives it a different shape, sustains the tone, and makes it more consistent. Dynamics layering can be time-consuming, so it is often overlooked. If you are presented with a sound containing a fast attack, you may need to layer it with another sound with a long release or slow attack. This will help eradicate transient build-up, at the same time, giving clarity to your sound. The possibility of clipping and distortion is also reduced.

**Stereo field**: Stereo should be your last consideration. Why? Because it can mask a poorly layered sound, but if you are able to carry out the first two successfully, achieving stereo should be very easy. Sound can only be panned to the left or right of the stereo field, or you can either increase or reduce the stereo width using a stereo-imaging plugin.

**Sound Layering Tips**

❖ Be prepared to remove or replace sounds that are not working for your layers; in simple words, don't get too attached.

❖ Less is better, minimize as much as possible the number of your layers. This does not imply that you can't stack more than five sounds together, but if there is a layer available that can perform the work of two or more layers, be sure to use it.

❖ Thinner sounds are better for layering.

❖ Make a habit out of re-pitching your sounds, as it helps two or more sound to gel even before the addition of effects.

❖ Be sure to avoid repetition, use different combinations of layers.

# Chapter Eight: Recording

The recording is exciting for those already familiar with it, if you've ever been to a recording studio and observed the way a professional works around the instrument, you will admit, it's quite fascinating, his interaction with the mixing board, pushing a button here and there. You can't just start recording with any type of mixer, the choice of your mixer depends on the type of instrument accessible to you in your studio and your budget.

## Three Basic Types of Recording Systems

**Studio-in-a-box (SIAB) system**: this is an all in one unit that comes with a digital mixer, most mixers in this category are quite easy to navigate, you only need to plug in your instrument or your microphone, and you are good to go. This category of mixers is flexible in routing signals, allowing you to achieve much with little to no hassle. Although the mixers in each SIAB system vary in terms of specification and features, so before you get one of these, make sure to check if it has your desired feature.

**Computer-based system**: All recording software comes with their own digital mixer that is controlled by your keyboard and mouse. This software also allows you to access an external bit of hardware known as Computer Control Surface (CCS), which lets you work with physical knobs and sliders. The CCS can be handy, especially when you decide to use a computer-based Digital Audio Workstation and want to control the virtual mixer with some hardware. While the computer control surface performs the function of a digital mixer, not all computer control surface is compatible with each software, so before you get the computer control software, check to see if it is compatible with your system.

**Stand-alone components**: In this system, everything is separate. Here, you need to buy a mixer before you can make use of your recorder. But the advantage of this system is that you get to choose between an analog or digital mixer. Also, you get to choose your cords, and as these are essential for the proper connection, it can be quite expensive.

## Mixers

The mixer is very important equipment in recording, and the more familiar you are with it, the easier it is for you to produce music. It gives you control over a variety of input and output configurations. Picture your mixer as a traffic controller communicating with different units to make the traffic move faster and avoid a collision. They route all signals, both incoming and outgoing coming from the instrument and recording device and make sure they get to their desired destination without a hitch. Understanding the mixer encompasses the input, trim control, and the channel strip. The moment you are well versed in their functions and how they operate, then operating a mixer becomes an easy feat to achieve.

## Understanding Signal Flow in Recording

The movement of signals within your system is one of the essential things to remember when recording. You will appreciate having this knowledge as it helps you to create music exactly as you envisioned it in your head. Here is how a signal moves through your channel strip:

**Source Audio or Input**: This is the signal coming from your hardware input or record, or the signal recorded on your hard drive. Your signal originates from your audio source and moves to the channel strip.

**Insert:** This function allows you to insert effects such as equalizer and dynamic processors when there is a need to change the sound of the entire signal.

**Send Pre Fader**: This function allows you to route part of your signal out to an Aux bus where effect such as reverb can then be inserted. With effects like reverb, you would want to control how much of the effects you can hear since it's only a part of the signal you are dealing with and not the entire portion. To achieve this function, you adjust the knob or slide to send as much or as little of the signal to the right Aux component.

**Send Postfader**: When your pre button has been disengaged, your track passes through the track fader from where a signal is sent.

**Pan**: This button allows you to adjust the amount of signal going to the left or right of a channel connected to the stereo output.

**Output**: This is the destination of your signal as it leaves the track channel strip, it can be a master bus, an aux, or a semi bus (from where it is then directed to the master bus).

### Understanding Mixer Routing

Routing or Busing can simply be explained as the process of sending a signal obtained from an instrument connected to the channel strip out to where it can be processed. The first stop of the signal when it is sent out is a bus. There are three types of buses that can receive a signal

➤ Master bus

➤ Aux bus

➤ Submix bus

## Master Bus

This is where your song is actually being mixed. From the master bus, you can choose which physical output the signal would be sent to. The pan button on the channel strip allows you to know the amount of signal sent either to the left or right of the stereo field. The master bus has its own dedicated channel strip, which is a stripped-down version of the regular one that allows you to add special effects such as compression and EQ. The master bus channel strip does not have a routing option such as input selection, solo, and mute button. This is because you are in the final stage of your signal flow, so you don't really need them. Remember, the fader in each channel is used to control the level of the signal sent to the master bus and the volume level of each signal; therefore, the master fader is used to determine the overall volume of all channels that are routed to it before it is sent to a desirable output device.

## Aux Bus

This is where your signal goes to when one of the send function is being used on the channel strip. Aux bus also has a dedicated channel strip of its own, where you can insert some desirable effects such as reverb. When you are done with the changes you need to make, the next stop of the signal is the master bus. There it can mix with the other signals that make up your track.

## Sub-Mix Bus

Sometimes, you may want to control a group of instruments independent of the master fader. To do this, you can create a group for the track and sub-mix them so you can adjust the volume without affecting the other instruments that are not in the group. The process is called Submixing, and the signal is sent to the sub-mix bus. From the sub-mix bus, the signal moves to the master bus, where it is blended with signals coming from other tracks. In the case of software mixers that are not in possession of a sub-mix bus, you can perform this function by simply routing your signal to any internal buses; from there, you can adjust the level using the channel strip fader associated with the internal bus.

**Output Jacks**

Mixers contain a couple of output jacks that are located at the back of your hardware. There are different types of output jacks in a mixer;

**Monitor Jack**

The monitor jack has the same signal as that of the master out jack and headphone jack but provides another space where a speaker or headphone can be plugged. It can also be used for Hardware monitoring on systems that have it; this is majorly common with a computer-based audio interface. It enables you to monitor the signal from the audio interface, instead of the signal going to the computer and back out before it reaches your ear – it reduces the latency that is heard when listening to yourself as you record.

**Master Out Jack**

It goes to the power amp of your speaker or directly to any powered monitors if you have one. It is controlled by the master fader.

## Phone Jack

This output jack is solely for your headphone, and it is fed by the phone knob of the master control. It carries the same signal as that of the master bus, but with the phone jack, you can control the volume separately.

## Microphones

This often the first device in a recording chain. A mic is a transducer that changes one form of energy to another, and in this case, the sound wave is transformed into an electrical signal. The quality a microphone picks up is often influenced by a number of external variables like the placement, acoustic environment, and distance or dependent on the design, which can be type, characteristics, or quality. The primary function of a microphone is to capture sound, but it can also be used to infuse a particular sound tone into a performance. There is also the preamp that helps boost the signal as it travels through the recorder. The combination of the two can help create a distinct sound or add a certain texture to your sound.

## Miking Technique

It has already been established that microphones are important devices in recording, so also is their placement. Some microphones will get you your desired sound when they are placed in a particular way.

There are four types of miking techniques, and each will be discussed in this chapter

1. Spot miking

2. Ambient miking

3. Distant miking

4. Stereo miking

## Spot Miking

Spot miking, also known as close miking, involves placing your microphone 1-3 feet within the sound source. This is done because sound diminishes with each square meter; it moves from the sound source. Spot miking creates a tight, present sound, and it is able to exclude the acoustic environment. This technique is mostly favored by home recordists because it adds a little of the room to the recorded sound. A disadvantage of spot miking is that it tends to create a less natural sound, and if you are not careful, it will compromise the quality of your recording.

## Factors to Consider when Using Spot Miking

Spot miking picks up more of transient materials, which can make your recording sound harsh. Whenever you are using spot miking for a transient instrument, move the mic back a bit or slightly point it away from the sound source.

Spot miking can be used to isolate many instruments on your track, and this will make your mixing process easier.

## Ambient Miking

This technique requires placing the mic at a distance far enough for it to capture the room sound (reverb and delay). The room sound can be equally or more prominent than the direct sound source. The mic is placed a few feet away from the sound source but pointed in the opposite direction to the sound. But in doing this, you cannot capture the attack of the instrument, so to overcome this effect, use a spot mic for the instrument. After recording, blend the sounds from both mics during the mixing process.

Another factor you need to consider is the room, does it have a good sound? If not, you are better off using only the spot-miking technique. The best place to use the ambient miking technique is when the room has a good sound, such that when it is mixed with spot mic, it creates a natural reverb. Also, in a live concert, the ambient mic can be placed over the audience to pick up their reactions.

### Distant Miking

This involves placing the mic 3-4 feet away from the sound source. This technique can capture part of the room's sound and that of the instrument as well, creating a tonal balance. Distance miking can be used for an entire instrument ensemble, for example, the drum set. Ambient mic, coupled with a spot mic, will help create a natural sound, but the pickup relies heavily on the acoustic environment. The mic should be placed at a distance that will help create a tonal balance. With the distant technique, your recording can have a live feeling to it, but the downside of this is that if your acoustic environment is not good enough, it reflects in your recording and will result in a muddy sound. To overcome this, you can place your mic closer to the source and add a degree of artificial ambiance.

### Stereo Miking

This technique involves the use of two microphones to capture a coherent stereo image. This technique can be applied to distant or spot miking of a single instrument. There are several stereo miking techniques, and they are:

➤ X/Y

➤ Spaced pair

➤ Mid side (M/S)

➤ Decca technique

➤ Blumlein pair


## X/Y Pair

The X/Y coincident stereo miking involves placing two mics of the same type, same manufacturer and model next to each other such that their diaphragm is so close without touching each other. The two mics face each other at angles between 900 and 1350, with the mid-point pointing outward towards the sound source. Nowadays, you can easily purchase a microphone with two diaphragms in the same casing. They are designed to allow the top diaphragm to rotate at 1800, allowing for adjustment of X/Y angles, or they can be fixed at angle 900.

## Space Pair

This involves placing two mics at a distance range of several feet to 30 feet from the instrument or ensemble. The major disadvantage to this technique is the tendency of phase discrepancy to occur, and when mixed in mono, this phase discrepancies lead to variation in frequency response.

## Mid- Side (M/S)

This is another coincident-pair system that is similar to the X/Y technique. The only difference is that it requires the use of a software plug-in, an external transformer, or an active matrix to work. In this technique, one mic, usually a cardioid mic, is designated as M (mid), which faces the sound source while the second mic is a bi-directional mic, designated as S (side). S is positioned perpendicular to M; therefore, M picks up sound directly from the source while S captures ambient and reverberant sound.

## Decca Pair

This technique is mainly used for recording classical, orchestra, and large ensembles. It consists of three omnidirectional mics in which two mics are placed three feet apart (one to the right and the other to the left), while the third one is placed about 1.5 feet to the front. The three mics are panned to match their configuration.

## Blumlein Pair

This is also similar to the X/Y pattern, but the difference is that the two bi-directional mics are placed at angle 900 to each other with the diaphragm as close as possible. The advantage is that the bi-directional mic is able to pick up sound from the front and back, creating a natural sound.

## Mic Placement for Different Instruments

Some mics work better in certain situations than others. This is due to the characteristics of some mic that allows them to be better equipped for a particular instrument. For instance, a condenser mic is better suited for an orchestra, where you want to pick everyone's voice, than a dynamic mic.

Choosing the best mic for your instrument or vocal depends on the type of sound you are aiming for, whether it is Punchy (which your best choice is the dynamic mic), mellow -which ranges from clear to croony, depending on the distance involved (the best choice is ribbon mic).

## Vocals

The human voice is a versatile sound source ranging from a shout to a whisper. There are different dynamics and timber in it, but generally, most people prefer a large-diaphragm condenser for vocals. Note that the choice depends on the sound you are aiming for. When you are in need of a dirty or raw sound, or in another case, there is a need for the singer to scream; then a dynamic mic should be your choice of the mic. But if you are aiming for a light sound, then the small diaphragm condenser mic should be your choice. Also, when you are miking for backup, the omnidirectional mic may be your choice as the singer can stand around it.

## Acoustic Guitar

It is characterized by a set of rich overtones. Mic placement for an acoustic guitar varies and may require experimentation to get the best type of microphone and placement. For optimum pickup:

The mic can be placed at 6-18 inches away from the guitar, and 3-4 inches below the point where the neck meets the body of the instrument.

You can also place the mic 3 feet away and point it directly to the soundhole; this captures the rich sound coming directly from the soundhole and the string.

Generally, for an acoustic guitar, you need a condenser mic, but if your intention is to get a richer sound, then a ribbon mic is the best choice. Your mic placement can be three inches to a foot or more depending on the type of sound you intend to get.

Also, for a louder instrument, choose a condenser mic or shift the mic away from the particular instrument a bit.

## Electric Guitar

Once again, the type of miking depends on the sound you are trying to achieve. If your aim is to get a distorted rock sound for your electric guitar, then a dynamic mic will help you achieve this. A small condenser mic can also help accomplish this feat. Sometimes, the type of mic used does not matter, but the placement of the mic does, and to get the best sound from your guitar amp, the mic has to be placed 2-12 inches from the amp cabinet, with the mic pointing directly to the cone of the amp. For speakers, sometimes a slight shift to the left or right is all it takes to achieve your sound.

After performing the procedure above, if you are still not getting your desired sound, you can add a second mic 3-4 feet away or point the mic directly at the speaker cabinet to produce an ambient sound.

## Electric Bass Guitar

Miking an electric bass guitar can be a real thorn in your side as it is very easy for the sound to be muddy and thin at the same time. You might think it is not possible for a sound to lack definition and be thin at the same time, but it does happen. To avoid this, you can run your bass guitar into the board through a direct box, Hi-Z, or an amp line out jack on the mixer; this helps a punchier sound.

Due to their low frequency, a dynamic mic or a large-diaphragm mic is the best option. When setting up the mic, it should be placed at 2-12inches away from its amp speaker, or you can angle the mic and let the speaker sound drift past the mic diaphragm.

**Piano**

Recording a piano sound can be tough, especially if the acoustics of your room is not so great. Due to the piano's size, you need a large room with high ceilings to record it. When piano sounds, the best type of mic to use is the condenser mic, whether it is a large-diaphragm mic or a small one, but getting your desired sound depends on its placement. If you are aiming for a natural classical sound, your mic should be placed 2-6 feet away from the instrument, depending on the amount of room sound you want in the mix. Remember, the farther away your instrument is to the mic, the more room sound it picks up.

Mic placement for a piano also depends on the type. For example, the grand piano which is an acoustically complex instrument can be miked in different ways depending on your preference, because of its size, a minimum distance of 4-6 feet is required a well-developed tonal balance and full pick-up. Sometimes, this is not feasible due to leakage from other instruments. Usually, when miking a grand piano, a condenser or dynamic mic is the preferred choice, but if there is a problem of excessive leakage from other instruments, then your best option is a closed-mike cardioid. There are several positions where a mic can be placed on the grand piano.

Position 1: a boundary mic is attached to the partially or entirely open lid.

Position 2: two mics are placed at a working distance of 1-6 inches, one is positioned over the low string while the other over the high string, using the stereo spaced pair configuration.

Position 3: a mic is placed inside the piano between the soundboard and the partially open lid.

Position 4: two mics are placed outside the lid in the stereo pair configuration.

Position 5: a single mic is placed over the piano hammer at a working distance of 4-8 inches.

For the upright piano, the miking technique is different from the grand piano since the former is designed for home enjoyment. There are different methods of miking an upright piano.

Method 1: miking over the top

The two mics are placed in a spaced fashion, one over the piano and the other in front of the piano's opened top. You can reduce resonance by angling the piano away from the wall.

Method 2: placing mic over the upper soundboard area

The mic is placed about 8inches from the soundboard, above both the bass and high string. This helps reduce excessive hammer attack.

## Drum Set

Getting your drum to sound fantastic depends on the type of sound you want. The first step to getting a good drum sound is proper tuning and a good head. When you invest time in selecting head and proper tuning, you are already halfway to getting a good sound; mic placement only contributes little to achieve this.

**Kick drum**: When recording a kick drum, the best mic is a dynamic mic. Some dynamic mic is specially designed for the kick drum. The mic can be placed halfway within the drum.

**Snare drum**: For the snare drum, the best option is a Cardioid pattern mic due to its location to other drums, especially the hi-hats. The mic is placed between the small tom-tom and the hi-hat about 1-2 inches from the snare head. This gives a punchy sound. For a crisper sound, add a second mic under the drum, placed at 1-2 inches from the head with the diaphragm pointing to the snare.

**Hi-hat**: For the hi-hat, a dynamic mic or a small diaphragm condenser mic is the best option. The dynamic mic gives a trashier sound while the condenser gives a bright sound. Both can be adjusted using EQ; the mic should be placed 3-4 inches above the hi-hat and pointed downwards. For hi-hats, the placement of the mic does not matter unlike that of the other instruments because of the tone, but be careful that your mic is not touching the hi-hat.

Most times, people don't mic the hi-hat because of the sound. But there are a lot of ways to mic the hi-hat. The first one is placing the mic on top of the cymbal; this will pick up the sound, or you can place the mic at the edge of the hi-hat and angle it in a way that is slightly below or slightly above the meeting point of the cymbals.

And if you are in a situation where there is only one mic, you can place it in between the hi-hat and the snare drum, facing it away from the rack tom as much as possible.

**Tom-tom:** The best mic for the tom-tom is the dynamic mic. For the rack tom (the one mounted above the kick drum), you can use one or two mics. In the case of one mic, place it between the two drums 4-6 inches away from the head, and if there are two mics available, place it 1-3-inches above each drum. The miking of small tom is similar to rack tom.

Miking the entire drum kit: Sometimes, there is a need for an overhead ambiance mic. If for no other reason than to pick up the high-transient sound of the cymbal. The best mic option for this is the ribbon or condenser mic (both large and small diaphragm), but preferably the latter because of its accurate high-end response. Condenser mic can pick up the high cymbal frequency and also give the drum sound at a certain brightness. For overhead miking, you can use one or two mics but preferably two. There are two techniques for overhead miking; they are:

➢ X-Y coincident technique

➢ Stereo pair technique

For the two techniques, the mic should be placed 1-2 feet above the cymbal. The X-Y mic should be placed at the center, just forward of the drummer's head, while for the stereo pair technique, the mics should be placed 3-6 feet apart and then pointed downward, towards the drum set.

**Hand drums**: the type of mic used, and placement depends on the drum itself and the tonal characteristics. For instance, the conga has a mid-range frequency and produces a large sound. So the best mic option is a condenser mic that can be able to capture the sound. Miking a hand drum also depends on the sound you want, if you are aiming for a tighter and drier sound, you can use a dynamic mic.

For the smaller high-pitch drums, it is preferable to use a condenser mic (both small and large-diaphragm) than a dynamic mic. Generally, for all hand drums, the mic should be placed 1-3 feet from the drum.

# Chapter Nine: Mixing

What is mixing? Mixing is the process whereby a multi-track material is blended, treated, and combined into a multi-channel format. The multi-track material can be a record, a sample of the synthesized material. But in the advance sense, it simply means recording and blending tracks together through several processes to make it sound cohesive and balanced. A mix is the sonic representation of creative ideas, performance, and the emotions you are trying to project. A mix can be a factor that will determine the success of your album. The main aim of mixing is to turn a different track into a homogenous mixture.

## Characteristics of a Good Mix

• **Balance**: The different frequency bands should be in a balanced proportion with each other. Also, it should have a left-right balance.

• **Clarity**: Even though the aim is for the track to blend together, it is still important for each instrument to be heard. In a good mix, you should be able to identify the kick drum and the bass as a separate part.

• **Emphasis**: The hook of a song should be attractive without having any mastering and mixing tricks.

• **Multi-dimensionality**: A good mix should be able to give the impression that some instruments are placed in the front, while some are placed to the back, left and right.

### Listening

Listening is a very important skill to acquire in mixing. It may seem easy, but it is not. You need to develop ways to verify whether the sound you are hearing is truly what you are hearing. Over the years, in order to verify this, a lot of techniques have been developed.

## Some of the Techniques Developed are Discussed Below

● **Listen to multiple monitors**: This is very important, especially when you are trying to get the balance of a mix. Even though all your work can be done on a single monitor, it does not hurt to check your mix against other sources as well. Most mixers settle for a set of monitors they feel is right for their music, familiarize themselves with its strengths and weaknesses, while using another smaller set of speakers to check the balance. These monitors do not have to be the best; in fact, if the monitors are terrible, it is an advantage because the majority of the listeners may not have the quality of your own speaker, so you get to hear how they will hear the sound in the real world. These speakers can range from a computer extension speaker to earbuds. The main reason for this is to check whether one instrument is not too loud or too low. Balancing is also one of the main arts of mixing, especially getting the kick drum and the bass guitar to sound well on a smaller monitor.

● **Listening in mono**: Since you will get to listen to your mix in mono, it is better to start as early as possible. Doing this helps a mixer to discern phase coherence, balancing, and even panning.

## Processes and Techniques Involved in Mixing

Before you start any mixing process, preparation for mixing is very important. Like the saying, proper preparation prevents poor performance. In mixing, it helps you avoid unnecessary mistakes and make your work easier.

Over the years, preparation for mixing has evolved. Once upon a time, preparing for mixing is about labeling your console and setting up your outboard gears, but today it is much more than that. It involves a series of processes like labeling your file and making your track layout within the DAW. Preparation for your mixing session can be carried out through the following steps:

➢ Make a session file copy

➢ Eliminate noise

➢ Tweak your track timing

➢ Check your fades

➢ Tune your track

➢ Comp your track

➢ Arrange your track

**Mechanism of Mixing: The Overall Approach**

Most mixers already have an idea of the final version of their mix before they even start mixing, so they take their time to familiarize themselves with the song first. Whether they are aware of it or not, most mixing engineers have their own approach to a mix, although this may vary depending on the song, artist, or genre. Their techniques are basic: determine what they want from the song, the direction, the feeling they want to generate, develop the groove, find the most important element in the mix and emphasize it. All these techniques are innate in most mixers such that they find themselves carrying out these processes without realizing they are following the pattern.

Three-dimensional mixing (tall, wide, and deep) is a characteristic common among great mixers.

The tall signifies frequency; all instruments involved in a mix have to balance frequency wise, i.e., all the frequencies must be properly represented.

The deep signifies the dimension. It is achieved by introducing ambiance elements to the mix through +reverbs, delays, and offshoots like chorusing. But this is not the only factor that gives depth to a mix; other factors include a mic, overheads, rooms, and leakage from other instruments.

The wide signifies panning; placing the audio element in the sound field must be able to create an interesting soundscape where all elements in the mix can be heard more clearly.

**Elements of a Mix**

There are six main elements to creating a great mix; they are:

● **Balance**: This is of the utmost importance; all the other elements pale in importance. It is the volume-level relationship between musical elements. Before you can create a good balance, your arrangement must be excellent. A good balance starts with a good arrangement. Arrangement in a mix is about tension, release, and dynamic changes such loud versus quiet, full versus sparse.

● **Dimension**: It involves adding ambiance to a musical element. It can be captured during recording, but creating or enhancing dimensions usually occur during mixing through the addition of effects like reverbs, modulation, and delay. Dimension is used to create an aural space, add excitement or add width and depth to a track.

● **Panorama element**: This is one of the elements of a mix that is commonly taken for granted. It involves placing the audio element in a sound field and understanding this element, and we must familiarize ourselves with the stereo system.

● **Frequency element**: The main tool here is the equalizer. It involves having all the frequency of an element well represented in the mix.

● **Dynamics**: Manipulation of dynamics, such as compression, limiting, plays a major role in sound. It involves the manipulation of the volume envelope of an individual track or the entire mix by increasing the level of soft sound and lowering the high one. This helps to keep the level of the sound in balance.

● **Interest**: this depends on you; it is what is added to make the mix special.

### Techniques for Mixing a Solo Project

➢ Know your aim for the mix: mixing starts even before you have an idea of the sound. You should have an idea of the element needed, the frequencies, and so on, even before you begin the mixing session. Also take your time to select sound and samples that will work well together, remember this matters a lot – your goal is for the element to sound well together and not as individual parts.

➢ Make use of Automation: Automation will help accentuate some parts, for example, when you need to slowly filter the bass during a build-up and then bring it back on the drop.

➢ Check your mix at different volume: it is better to mix at a lower volume, but does not to hurt to turn the volume up now and then. We hear different frequencies at different levels, so doing this will give you an overall idea of the sound.

➢ Use a reference track: select a professionally released track and use it to compare your own, remember the reference track will be louder than your own as it has been mastered, so make sure to bring the volume down.

➢ Be careful not to over-compress your mix: Compressing one instrument can make it sound better, but compressing a whole mix can give it a dull, flat sound that tires your ears.

# Chapter Ten: Mastering

Before you can fully create a piece of music, it has to go through several processes such as songwriting, recording, mixing, and finally mastering. It is the last step in the finalization of audio recording. In mixing, you work with individual tracks while in mastering, you work with the entire mix. Mastering is a combination of different processes that boil down to three primary processes – equalization, compression, and limiting. The aim is to ensure the best translation for your recording, i.e., brings out the best possible sound. Mastering is an art that has its own set of approaches and techniques.

## Advanced Techniques for Mastering

This section contains a wide array of techniques, some may be simple protocols to be observed, which are very crucial in your mastering processes, and some may help improve your work, while others prevent degradation. These techniques may be common or rare, but you can be able to choose what works for you and your music.

**Minimizing delay between comparisons**: there are instances when comparison will be made between an original version and a processed version, minimizing delay is important for absolute judgment. A common feature of DAW that helps you make a comparison is the solo mode. Particularly in mastering, the most common solo mode is exclusive, once you select exclusive and a track solo button is pressed, all other track will be un-soloed. But if the exclusive mode is not selected, a group of tracks is soloed, and this will not work if you are making an instant comparison.

**How to avoid ear fatigue**: Studies have shown that there are two types of ear fatigue, the short term and the long term. You can easily recover from short term ear fatigue under two minutes; this is why mastering engineers take short breaks in between sessions and before making any final decisions. Long term ear fatigue may be a result of long-term exposure to sound about 75dBSPL and above, so be careful not to expose your ears to such loudness.

**Stem mastering**: this is mastering performed from sub-mixes called the stem. The aim of stem mastering is to minimize some sacrifices made during mastering, for example, cutting or raising of bass frequencies only in the stem where the bass instrument is present instead of doing this for the entire mix. Stem mastering is a good option when the mastering environment is not conducive or when there are significant problems with no particular solution.

**Reverb processing**: Reverb should not be used on a professional production unless there is a need for significant depth. When you are working with this type of trouble mix, the first step is to try a remix, and if this does not work, you can add subtle high-quality reverb. The most basic way to approach this is to use a reverb processor coupled with a transient processor over the entire mix. This way, the punch will be intact with little reduction. In mastering, whenever Reverb is to be used, the reverb pre-delay settings, which will delay the reverb signal, is adjusted to achieve the best result. Doing this will help reduce the masking of the main signal by the reverb signal.

**Processing song section separately**: earlier, we learned that mastering deals with the entire mix, so it involves finding settings that work for the entire song. Sometimes a problem may arise in a particular section such that there will be a need for the said section to be processed separately. Sometimes, removing a single click or pop can lead to you destructively editing a small piece, probably even saving a new version of the change. The repair edits are often carried out in the waveform view of many DAWs. But if there is a problem with an entire section, it can be cut into separate parts and processed, after which you edit the parts back together; if the processing involves phase shift, it can lead to a problem in timing. This may be an anomaly in the beginning or end of an edit; careful editing can easily address this problem.

**Reference recording**: Reference recording are popular recordings of the highest quality with which is used for comparison with the recording being mastered. Most professionals have their own collection of reference recordings, or they can ask their clients to submit a reference recording that will give them insight into their client's taste. You can be able to capture your client's sonic vision through their reference recording; sometimes, it helps you reset your ear and perception while giving you a sense of balance. Reference recording can be an audio CD or a digital file that can be loaded into the DAW or played on a separate device. The best way to store a reference recording on the hard drive is through FLAC format. This will help preserve the original quality of the reference track.

**Mono compatibility**: it is crucial to listen to how your recording sounds when converted to mono. It has been said that listening to a recording with a car stereo is like listening to it in mono because of the arrangement of the speaker. Many DAWs and mastering console comes with features that enable you to listen to your recording in mono.

# Chapter Eleven: Manufacture and Distribution/Format

## The Digital World in Music

The digital world has played a major role in the music industry. The ever-evolving technology has changed the way music is manufactured and distributed today. It facilitates the means of producing and distributing music at a low cost. Nowadays, it is easier to produce music in the comfort of your room with just simple equipment, all thanks to digital technology.

### Multimedia and Web

Nowadays, the modern-day computers are much faster with multi-functional abilities. Not only do they make our work easier, but they have also been able to integrate media and networking into their functions as well. But in the real sense, multimedia is a unified programming and operating system. This system allowed multiple forms of program data to be stream and routed simultaneously to the appropriate hardware port for processing.

### Delivery Media

In media, data can be transmitted over a wide range of storage device; there are three major delivery media:

### CD

This compact disk is one of the important formats used in the distribution and marketing of music. It is in two forms, CD-ROM and CD-audio. The CD-ROM is capable of storing 700mb of graphics, digital audio, text, and raw data while its audio counterpart can store up to 74 minutes of audio.

## DVD

They are capable of storing up to 8.5 gigabytes of data on the double-layer disc and about 4.7 gigabytes on the single-sided disc. This capacity makes it the perfect delivery medium for DVD-Audio. They can contain any form of data.

## Web

One major aspect of multimedia is the ability to transmit data or information to either an individual or to the masses. And this is achieved through a network connection. The largest and common connection is the connection to the internet. The internet is a complex communication system that allows your computer to be connected to the internet service provided while an internet browser transmits and receives information via a uniform resources locator address.

## Audio Format

The delivery format is very important, especially when you are creating content for the media system. Your bandwidth requirement and format should be compatible with your content delivery system. Some of the formats of delivery are outlined below;

**Uncompressed sound file format**: they are bulky and occupies large space on your hard disk or any storage drive, but the main advantage of this format is that it maintains the quality of the digital audio stored on it, in other words, the quality of your audio remains unchanged no matter the number of times you process or encode it. An example of this is WAV format, AIFF format.

**Compressed sound file format**: one main advantage it has over the uncompressed format is that it makes more space available on your hard drive or any storage device, this is because it compresses the digital audio data leading to small file, but a major disadvantage is that it can lead to loss of data. The compressed sound file format can further be classified into two groups:

**Lossless compressed audio format**: in this format, your digital audio file is compressed to a smaller file, but the compression process does not result in loss of data or degradation in audio quality. A good example of this is the FLAC format.

**Lossy compressed audio format**: this format compress digital audio data, but the process eliminates some information and frequency to reduce the size. This results in a reduction of quality, which can be large or small depending on the amount of data that was eliminated. Subsequent processing will lead to more data loss. An example of this is MP3.

### Commonly Used Audio Format

**WAV format**: This stores uncompressed audio data with 100% data quality retention. It is mainly based on the RIFF bitstream format of storing data since it retains the original quality of data; it is popular among audio experts, and also editing can be done using software and commonly used on Windows systems.

**AIFF (Audio interchange file format) Format**: was developed by Apple computers and can also store uncompressed audio data, commonly used on the Apple Macintosh system, this format is also popular among professionals.

**MP3 format**: this format reduces the size of a file by eliminating some information through psychoacoustic compression and perspective audio coding. It can retain a larger percentage of the quality of the original data. It is commonly used to store a large number of songs on the computer as it will not take up much space but never record in MP3 unless there is absolutely no other option. Always make sure your recording is in an uncompressed format like WAV or AIFF, you may decide to convert it to MP3 format.

**FLAC (Free Lossless Audio Codec):** this format reduces the size of your audio file but still maintains the quality of the original data.

**AAC (Advanced Audio Format):** unlike its MP3 counterpart, it offers better quality than the MP3 at a smaller size. It is the audio format being used by Apple's iTunes.

**WMA (window media Audio) format**: in this format, you can encode high-quality audio at a reduced size. A major advantage of this format is that it is able to reproduce the original quality with no elimination of data similar to WAV.

How do I choose the best recording format?

In choosing the best recording format, there are two factors to consider, sampling rate and bit rate.

**Sampling rate**: this is the number of samples received per second. Audio signals are broken into samples that are received by your device e.g., computer during recording. The sampling rate is measured in hertz; it allows you to listen to uninterrupted audio playback. The higher the sampling rate, the greater the audio quality. The standard sampling rate for CD is 44.1 kHz.

**Bit rate**: the number of bits processed per unit of playback time is referred to as bit rate. While the sample rate represents the number of samples recorded overtime, bit rate represents the quality of each individual sample recorded. The higher the bit rate, the higher the quality of your audio, but the larger space it will occupy on your hard drive. Most studio prefers their bit rate to be 24, 32 or more; this is because there is more accuracy with your data, and this important for mixing and mastering process.

## Surround Sound

Surround sound started in the theatre; incorporating this technique into your speaker system will help enrich the depth and fidelity of your sound. Surround sound is designed to create a sound filed around you and also able to recreate the sound above you.

Ideally, a surround sound is made up of five speakers and a subwoofers, and if the room is long, then it requires seven speakers and a subwoofers, three speakers are installed along the front wall; one to the right, one to the left and the other at the center, one or two pairs of speakers are installed at the rear wall, thereby surrounding you with sound in all direction.

## Monitor Placement in Surround Sound

The monitor of choice for your surround sound depends on the level of quality, functionality, and cost. All these factors must be taken into account before choosing a monitor. Another important factor to consider is how you plan to monitor in surround. Does your console or DAW offer true monitor surround capabilities? If they do, then you are lucky, and if they don't, you will need a hardware surround monitor control system or a surround preamp. Take your time to research and decide the type of surround mastering tool that will be best for your music; Mixing and mastering in surround can be a real challenge, when you considered all the factors and have made your decision, you can then go ahead to install a 5.1 surround system.

The 5.1 monitor set-up is made-up of five full-range speakers arranged in a circular arc with the speakers at equal distance from a center position. Three speakers at the front, as explained earlier with the center speaker being placed at dead center 0o from the center point and the other two (the one on the left and right) being placed at 30o arcs of the speaker at the center. The remaining two are at 110o at the rear from the center point. The subwoofer should be placed near the dead center. Also, active subwoofers offer full control over gain and crossover frequency. All the surround monitors should be gain-adjusted in order to be able to deliver the same sound output level.

The surround system makes use of bass management to low route frequency to the subwoofers. The subwoofers channel is called ".1" because the range is limited to bass frequency alone. A major advantage of bass management is that it takes much load off the speakers, so they can sound louder with little to no distortion as they don't have to produce bass frequencies.

# Chapter Twelve: Predictions

Through the years, sound technology has improved and is still improving. Two modern factors that have come into play are digital audio and the web. The ability to turn the digital 1's and o's into alphabetical words has been a turning point that has changed communication and creative production.

The advent of pc, DAWs, and digital downloads has not only made music production easy and cost-effective, but it also creates certain flexibility and an ideal environment for music production. Beyond all this is the World Wide Web; this has taken music to a new height. Music is not static; it is growing and evolving every day.

Music in the last few decades has witnessed the advent of file sharing to the invention of DAWs. But in the next coming decade, it would still undergo some more transformation. A few decades ago, before you can become an international star, you need a huge record label, millions of investment and still look the part, but nowadays, a lot of stars are born through the internet, and in the next couple of decades more stars will be born through this. This is because the internet, social media smartphone, coupled with internet speed streaming, will put a lot of artists into the limelight without the help of a record label. In the near future, record labels may be a thing of the past; the main function of a record label is marketing, distribution, and A&R.

In the past, labels would discover an artist and develop them to become a global sensation, but now the A&R function of a record label is being eradicated as artists are now signed on the strength of their streaming or social media followers, where there is an existing fan base for the label to utilize. Nowadays, there is little need for a record label in the distribution of music; anyone can distribute their music through a digital service provider for a token. It does not mean that record labels are not required; getting signed to a record label has its own advantage and privileges, but in the near future, there might not be a need for them anymore. Autonomous artists!

Soon, music will become more global and more localized, in the sense that more audiences would have access to music, even ones that are not in their original language. Meanwhile, artists who previously felt obliged to perform in English will start performing in their original language.

Soon, Artificial intelligence is going to be a turning point for the music industry, in fact, they are already changing it, with tools like A.I- mediated composition and voice synthesis, thousands of musician all over the world will be able to produce high-quality music by themselves and distribute at a lower cost.

# Conclusion

Before you can become a professional, you must have been a beginner at one point. At the beginner stage of your journey, you must have been on shaky ground, but transcending into a professional is all about solidifying and legitimizing your stance in the whole scheme of things, music production-wise, of course. A beginner who is ready to go pro must have acquired the necessary tools, technical knowhow, financial, and mental ability to be able to go the extra mile.

The assumption under which this book is compiled is that you already have considerable knowledge about what music production is all about, especially if you were opportune to read the beginner edition. Therefore, if the book was not basic enough for your taste, I apologize profusely. I tried as much as possible not to dictate/enforce exactly what to buy and use in terms of studio equipment, both hardware, and software, but rather provide information on the attributes you should look out for so that you have the opportunity to derive what works best for you.

A few of the issues tackled in the book are as follows but are not limited to it.

➢ The components of a professional music studio.

➢ The pro-DAW system.

➢ Professional music capable home recording studio.

➢ How a studio is to be designed.

➢ The importance of working together (collaboration).

- The importance of soundproofing.

- The rudiments of Acoustic treatment.

- Explicit discussion on some of the instruments used in the studio

- Professional roles in music production

- Structure and arrangement of hit songs

- The production process

- Predictions on what to expect in 2020, and many more.

A lot of emphases were made in the book about the importance of initially establishing both your long term and short-term goals, so you have a clear path to achieving them. Doing this makes you more focused, which increases the probability of you achieving your aims. The book also advocated that you should have a mentor (an authority in professional music production) whose footsteps you will adopt as a kind of blueprint to your own work.

Finally, in your struggle to attain professionalism, do not settle for just the ordinary or normal or status quo. Always strive to do your best at all times. Do not follow the trend blindly; rather, observe it and then manipulate it to suit your perspective. At the end of it all, your efforts will be crowned with the production of not just great recordings but unique ones too. Takes this advice with you as a parting gift; Practice and hard work are never too much. The so-called seasoned professional still make errors; therefore, what excuse do you have?

# Discover "How to Find Your Sound"

## http://musicprod.ontrapages.com/

## Swindali music coaching/Skype lessons.

Email djswindali@gmail.com for info and pricing

# References

https://www.renegadeproducer.com/music-production-techniques.html

https://www.musicradar.com/tuition/tech/19-sequencing-and-midi-power-tips-191594

https://www.audio-issues.com/home-recording-studio/demystifying-audio-formats-what-format-should-you-record-in/

https://www.musicradar.com/tuition/tech/12-sound-layering-tips-and-tricks-589568

https://www.waves.com/six-stages-of-music-production

https://en.m.wikipedia.org/wiki/Mixing_engineer

https://www.careersinmusic.com/

https://www.techwalla.com/articles/the-difference-between-subwoofers-speakers

https://musiccritic.com/equipment/speakers/10-best-studio-monitors-speakers/

https://iconcollective.edu/best-studio-desks/

https://www.musiciansfriend.com/thehub/audio-mixers-how-to-choose

https://www.musiciansfriend.com/thehub/usb-microphone-buying-guide

https://www.thebalancecareers.com/what-is-a-sound-engineer-2460937

https://www.tunecore.com/blog/2018/05/how-to-write-produce-hit-song-in-2018.html

https://www.hitsongsdeconstructed.com/

Using a professional music recording studio can make a difference in your career, here's why

https://www.tunedly.com/blogpost?blog=WhyUseaProRecordingStudio?

The recording engineer and other roles found in the studio

https://www.practical-music-production.com/recording-engineer/

How to collaborate effectively with other music producers

https://www.izotope.com/en/learn/how-to-collaborate-effectively-with-other-music-producers.html#person

Collaboration: how your music can benefit from producing with others

https://www.edmprod.com/collaboration/

How to soundproof a room for audio recording

https://www.adorama.com/alc/how-to-soundproof-a-room-for-audio-recording

How to soundproof a room for music (Listening and Recording)

https://aquietrefuge.com/soundproof-room-for-music/

Music Collaboration: How-To and Why

https://www.musicgateway.com/blog/how-to/music-collaboration-how-to-best-music-collaboration-sites

How to build a recording studio

https://www.planetarygroup.com/music-promotion-guide/build-recording-studio/

Top 10 DAW recording software 2020

https://musiccritic.com/equipment/software/best-daw-recording-software/

Audio production

https://www.audiomentor.com/audioproduction/how-to-choose-a-daw

The acoustic treatment for panels & foam

https://ledgernote.com/columns/studio-recording/acoustic-treatment-guide-for-panels-and-foam/

The complete recording studio equipment list

https://ehomerecordingstudio.com/recording-studio-equipment-list/

Modern Recording Techniques 7th and 8th editions by David Miles Huber

The Music Business and Recording Industry 3rd Edition by Geoffrey P. Hull, Thomas Hutchison, and Richard Strasser.

The Mixing Engineer's Handbook 3rd edition by Robby Owsinski.

Modern recording techniques by David Miles Huber

Home recording for musicians for dummies by Jeff Strong

Complete guide to audio mastering by Gebre Waddell

The mixing engineer's handbook by Bobby Owinski